Character Education in America's Schools

Terri Akin
Gerry Dunne
Susanna Palomares
Dianne Schilling

Innerchoice Publishing, Torrance, California

Cover Design: Doug Armstrong Graphic Design

Copyright © 1995, Innerchoice Publishing • All rights reserved

ISBN: 1-56499-026-5

INNERCHOICE PUBLISHING
P.O. BOX 1185
TORRANCE, CALIFORNIA 90505
Tel. (310) 816-3085 Fax (310) 816-3092

Handouts may be reproduced in quantities sufficient for distribution to students in classrooms utilizing *Character Education in America's Schools*. All other reproduction, for any purpose whatsoever, is explicitly prohibited without written permission. Requests for such permission should be directed to INNERCHOICE PUBLISHING.

Contents

Introduction 1

An Overview of the Sharing Circle 9

Instructional Units 19

    Trustworthiness 19

    Respect 37

    Responsibility 57

    Justice and Fairness 77

    Caring 95

    Citizenship 113

    Moral Reflection 131

Literature Connection 161

A society needs values education both to survive and to thrive — to keep itself intact, and to keep itself growing toward conditions that support the full human development of all its members. These days, when schools don't do moral education, influences hostile to good character rush in to fill the values vacuum.

—Thomas Lickona

A teacher affects eternity.
—John Adams

Introduction

Why Educate for Character?

Because many homes do not. The primary responsibility for instilling values rests in the home. Few of us would argue with that belief. But children are growing up without moral compasses, and the home is a big part of the problem. One-half of all children live in nontraditional families, including single-parent families and "blended" families, consisting of stepparents, grandparents, other relatives and nonrelatives. While many nontraditional environments are no doubt exceedingly healthy, statistics nonetheless link the decline of the traditional nuclear family with rising teen pregnancy, school drop-outs, divorce rates, unemployment, poverty, and just about every other ill in our society.

Meanwhile, in growing numbers of traditional families, both parents share the wage-earning role, and children spend many hours without parental supervision, often in front of the TV, where they suffer lethargy, sensory deprivation and eroding physical health while witnessing murder, mayhem, and some of the worst models of morality imaginable.

On-the-go, stretched-to-the-limit working parents are not finding the time — or perhaps the will, or the skills — to guide their children through the complex labyrinth of challenges they encounter on a daily basis and help them make reasoned decisions based on sound ethical and moral principles.

Because we don't just want smart kids, we want good kids. Education has always attempted to develop good people. Even during periods when teachers were told that they *must not* teach values, they did anyway. They modeled kindness, caring, and respect; punished cheating, stealing, and lying; rewarded industriousness; and emphasized the importance of good citizenship in the context of a just and fair school community.

Responsible behavior begins with ethical thinking, and helping students to think — to solve problems, make decisions and render judgments — is clearly the job of the school. Along with language, math, science, and art, schools must teach acceptable standards of conduct, and the attitudes and attributes that foster them. Smart is not enough to sustain the principles and belief systems upon which our society is built. Good, the estranged twin, belongs in this picture.

Because to some degree good comes before smart. To consistently do their best work, students must value excellence, even if it's just an excellent grade. Few students can do well in school without work, and work requires diligence. If every child came to school with well developed senses of responsibility, honesty, integrity, and fairness, teaching would be easy. But since, both practically and developmentally, this is impossible, schools are left with no choice but to instill values right along with the other basics. They always have. They always will. The difference is that today many schools are again teaching values deliberately — through the curriculum.

According to Lawrence Kohlberg and others who have done extensive research on moral development, elementary-age children are primarily concerned with their own survival — avoiding punishment and obtaining rewards by obeying the rules. Older children are motivated by the desire to gain approval from others (principally peers) and avoid disapproval. Only at the highest level of moral development are rules interpreted in terms of self-chosen principles.

The strong influence of the home in preschool years gives way to the broader world of the the school and peer group as children enter school. Educators are not usurping a family mandate by teaching moral values; the children carry the mandate with them, right out the door and into the school. They are whole people, and schools cannot deal with their minds apart from their morality.

Because somebody's got to do it. Knowing that so many children lack role models and caring adults in their lives, and knowing, as a consequence, that society is in real danger, the educational system would be negligent were it not to respond. To some, character education will seem like just one more job added to the teacher's overwhelming list of responsibilities. But it's a critically important job — and somebody's got to do it.

What Is Good Character?

In, *Educating for Character* (Bantam, 1991), psychologist and educator Thomas Lickona states that good character consists of "knowing the good, desiring the good, and doing the good — habits of mind, habits of heart, and habits of action." In other words, a morally mature person knows what is right, cares deeply about what is right, and does what is right. The following chart, adapted from Lickona's book, further breaks down these three components:

Moral Knowing
Awareness
— seeing the moral dimensions of life situations
Knowing moral values
— understanding of objectively worthwhile values
Perspective-taking
— empathy
Moral reasoning
— understanding why some actions are morally better than others
Decision making
— considering alternatives, consequences and the moral values at stake
Self-knowledge
— including capacity for self-criticism

Moral Feeling
Conscience
Self-esteem
Empathy
Loving the good
Self-control
Humility

Moral Action
Competence
— skills and the ability
Will
— intentionality
Habit

What Values Should We Teach?

Many teachers in classrooms today recall being told never to venture into the values arena under any circumstances. To those teachers, the current interest in character education must seem rather ironic. Does our concern for morality skip whole decades? What happened?

The short answer is this: While trying to meet the educational needs of an increasingly pluralistic society, educators went through a period of several years wherein no one was sure whose values to teach. With so many cultures, languages, and ethnic groups to accommodate, schools thought it best to leave the entire issue of values alone. Developing character was the job of families, supported by their religious institutions. Unfortunately, both families and religious institutions were losing their sway over young people during that same period of time.

Today, educators are not so worried about "whose values to teach," and are acknowledging that every person needs to acquire certain character attributes and be guided by universal moral values — values that unite all people everywhere because they affirm basic human worth and dignity.

Universal moral values underlie the 1948 United Nations Universal Declaration of Human Rights, which calls for:

- life
- liberty
- freedom from personal attack
- freedom from slavery
- recognition before the law and the presumption of innocence until proven guilty
- freedom from torture
- freedom of conscience and religion
- freedom of expression
- privacy, family, and correspondence
- freedom to participate freely in community life
- education
- a standard of living adequate for maintaining health and well being

The Aspen Conference

The activities in this book have been organized around six core universal moral values outlined by a group of twenty-nine youth leaders and educators at what has come to be known as the "Aspen Conference." Meeting in Aspen, Colorado, on July 22-25, 1992, the participants of the conference sought to define a brief yet comprehensive list of values that could serve as a "common denominator," uniting not only themselves, but all people and organizations in our society. The six core values, which are outlined in greater detail on the following page, are:

- **Trustworthiness**
- **Respect**
- **Responsibility**
- **Justice and Fairness**
- **Caring**
- **Civic Virtue and Citizenship**

Although neither endorsed by nor in any way affiliated with the Aspen Conference or its sponsors, the authors of this book have chosen to devote one unit of activities to each of these six core values. A culminating unit is comprised of activities that give students an opportunity to review the core values and to identify and discuss those that are relevant to a number of typical life situations. In addition, we have included a section entitled the "Literature Connection,"

The Six Pillars of Character

- **Trustworthiness**

Worthy of trust, honor, and confidence
    Honesty: trustful, sincere, nondeceptive, candid, not cheating
    Integrity: morally courageous, principled
    Promise-Keeping: dependable, reliable
    Loyalty: faithful, allegiant, supportive, maintains confidences

- **Respect**

Regard for dignity, worth and autonomy of all persons (including self)
    Treating others with courtesy, civility, politeness
    Tolerating others' beliefs
    Accepting individual differences without prejudice
    Refraining from violence, coercion, intimidation

- **Responsibility**

Acknowledgement and performance of duties to others and self
    Accountability: answerable for consequences of decisions
    Pursuit of Excellence: diligent, perseverant
    Self-discipline: self-control, restraint

- **Justice and Fairness**

Making decisions on appropriate factors: impartiality, avoidance of conflicts of interest
    Commitment to equity and equality
    Openness to information and ideas
    Reasonableness
    Due process
    Consistency
    Fair play

- **Caring**

Regard for the well-being of others
    Kindness
    Compassion
    Consideration
    Unselfishness
    Charity: altruism, giving

- **Civic Virtue and Citizenship**

Recognition of and living up to social obligations
    Participation in democratic process
    Law abidance
    Protection of environment
    Community service
    Doing one's share

Reprinted with permission from *Ethics: Easier Said Than Done,* The Josephson Institute of Ethics, ©1992, Issues 19 & 20, P. 80

What Schools Can Do

Everything about a school reflects to some degree that school's current set of values. The way administrators lead and teachers manage their classes, the way grades are awarded and sports programs are administered, the way hallways and playgrounds are monitored all send moral messages. These messages, picked up by students on super sensitive receivers, significantly affect character development.

Much of what students learn is learned by imitation or modeling. The younger the student, the stronger the impact of models on development. For this reason, the values that you choose to teach should extend to all aspects of school life.

The experiences generated by being a member of the school community are much more character-forming than anything an individual teacher can say on the subject of morality or ethics. Ask regularly: *What lessons are being taught by the way our school operates on a daily basis?*

Does your school...
1. have a philosophy statement clearly outlining character expectations for all members of the school community? Is it posted prominently and a visible part of school life? If you are a teacher, do you have a compatible philosophy statement for your classroom?

2. provide all students with clear academic and behavior goals?

3. have a discipline policy that supports the character goals of the school?

4. encourage students to participate in formal school and/or community service projects?

5. have available to students on a regular basis general school service activities, e.g., teacher aides, messengers, tutors, guest greeters, fundraising, school clean up, etc.?

6. have a range of extracurricular activities led by school staff and supported by parents and community, e.g., sports, band, choir, drama, art club, etc.?

Do you...
1. demonstrate character traits and pro-social habits that are supportive of the school philosophy and goals? Do other faculty, administrators, and certified staff also effectively model these goals and philosophy?

2. see a relationship between the way you treat students and the way they treat each other?

3. have an awareness of how small actions model and teach?

4. share concern for the well-being of others — both students and staff?

5. give extra help to students who need it?

6. educate enthusiastically?

7. come to your classes prepared to lead class activities?

8. return students work in a timely manner?

9. refrain from gossiping or criticizing students, parents, or administrators?

Service Learning

Through service learning, students participate in deliberate character-building experiences — systematic activities that result in real assistance to others, as well as personal growth. In the process, those activities reinforce specific values, such as responsibility, caring, and citizenship.

Many prosocial activities can be carried out by students in schools at all levels. Participating in service learning gives students opportunities to practice moral values and develop good character. Schools with many extracurricular activities and service opportunities almost always do a better job of developing student character.

Service learning programs should include:
- Training. Students who have never helped others may not know how. Train them in basic helping skills.
- Supervision. Help students adjust to new situations and continue to develop needed skills, while providing feedback, encouragement and motivation to continue.
- Ongoing support. Provide help with problem solving, encourage reflection, continue to motivate, and give plenty of recognition

Classroom Service Opportunities
aides
messengers
monitors
clean-up helpers
tutors
homework buddies
members of cooperative learning projects

School Service Opportunities
competitive sports
performing groups — band, choir, dramatics, forensics
fundraising
school newspaper
student council
academic competitions
school greeters and tour guides
conflict managers
safety patrol

Community Service Opportunities
building projects
community clean-up projects
recycling/re-use centers
day-care centers
retirement and nursing home visitations
at-home assistance for elderly

What Teachers Can Do

Moral values are already so tightly woven into the fabric of classroom life that we no longer see the individual threads. The environment of the classroom is rich with values. The question is: which values?

It is who we are more than what we say that builds character in children. Students learn from what they observe and experience in the environment; they develop the values that you model.

All students, and particularly at-risk students, need consistent caring in the form of support and encouragement. They must know that you believe they can overcome obstacles and that you are depending on them to make ethical, pro-social choices.

The Model:
- Treat students with love and respect; set a good example.
- Share your moral convictions with students.
- Talk about community service you perform.
- Establish clear academic and moral goals for your class.
- Present well-planned lessons.
- Teach enthusiastically.
- Return homework and test papers promptly.
- Don't gossip about students or colleagues.
- Show consideration for other teachers.
- Go the extra mile for a student who is struggling.

The Words
- State character goals as positive imperatives, e.g., "Be on time," "Treat others fairly," "Do your best work," "Keep your word." Avoid negative wording, such as "Don't be late," "Don't be unkind," and "Never break a promise."
- Teach values directly. Use the words (i.e., *trustworthiness, respect, responsibility, caring*, etc.), write and define them, identify the behaviors in which they are embodied, and have students practice those behaviors.

The Environment
- Help students know each other, respect and care about each other, and experience a sense of full inclusion in the group.
- Through cooperative learning, teach children to help each other and work together.
- Display pictures, portraits of worthy individuals, posters, and quotations that reflect the high moral purpose and goals of your class.
- Teach values in conjunction with parents and community.

The Management
- Use the creation and enforcement of rules as opportunities to foster moral reasoning.
- Instill civic values by holding class meetings to discuss problems that arise.
- Involve students in decision making and shared responsibility for making the classroom a positive place to learn.

The Skills
- Teach a decision-making process that encourages students to make conscious choices from among alternatives that have been examined not only for their relative effectiveness in achieving a stated goal, but for their moral consequences.
- Teach skills of listening, communication, assertiveness, problem solving, conflict resolution, and refusal/resistance.
- Give students many opportunities to make choices.

The Academics
- Use academic subjects as a vehicle for examining ethical issues.
- Foster academic responsibility and regard for the value of learning and work.
- Encourage moral reflection through reading, writing, discussion.
- Give students opportunities to respond to moral issues.

reading, writing, discussion.
- Give students opportunities to respond to moral issues.

How to Use This Book

As mentioned previously, the activities in *Character Education in America's Schools* are grouped into seven topic areas or units. The first six correspond to the core values, or "pillars of character," developed by the delegates at the Aspen Conference on character education. The seventh is a summary unit, designed to review and reinforce the concepts presented in the other six.

The activities within each unit are arranged in a logical, and to some extent developmental, sequence. However, in most cases you are not required to implement the activities in the order presented. In those rare cases where two activities are linked, the directions so indicate. The great majority of activities are completely independent and capable of standing on their own.

The activities in the summary unit ("Moral Reflection") will probably have the greatest impact if they are implemented after the students have examined each of the six core values in some depth. Keep in mind, however, that the final unit houses a number of stories and dilemmas. By all means take the liberty of dipping into those at any time. Simply adjust the discussion questions to the readiness of your students to deal with various concepts.

Additional modifications should be made to suit the ages, ability levels, cultural/ethnic backgrounds, and interests of your students. Suggested adaptations for younger students are already included at the end of many activities; however, you will know best how to maximize the appropriateness and impact of each experience, so please take those liberties.

At the conclusion of most activities, you will encounter a list of "Discussion Questions." Discussion questions are provided to help you involve students in thinking about and summarizing the learnings derived from a particular activity. They promote moral and ethical reasoning, the use of higher-level thinking skills, and internalization of knowledge and skills. When planning for implementation, always allow plenty of time for debriefing and discussion.

The final pages of the book are devoted to a special section called the "Literature Connection." The books annotated on these pages were selected because they relate directly to the six core moral values. You should have no trouble locating these titles; all are popular books, readily available through libraries and bookstores. Each of the entries is coded to indicate grade level — primary (P), intermediate (I), or upper (U).

The last four or five activities in each unit are Sharing Circles. A Sharing Circle is a small-group discussion characterized by a unique two-part structure (sharing followed by summary discussion) and prescribed rules of conduct that ensure acceptance, listening, safety, mutual respect, and confidentiality.

The Sharing Circle is an extremely powerful process for ethical and moral reflection. Part of its value for this purpose lies in the fact that it is guided by an established procedure and a specific topic. In addition, the process requires that students demonstrate respect, responsibility, trust, caring, and fairness as a condition of participating in every circle.

If you are new to Sharing Circles, please read the next section of this book thoroughly before leading your first one. Every Sharing Circle in the book also includes a list of "topic variations." Once you become comfortable with the process, you will be able to develop and lead your own circles with just a topic in mind.

An Overview of the Sharing Circle

The Sharing Circle is a unique small-group discussion process in which participants (including the leader) share their feelings, experiences, and insights in response to specific, assigned topics. Sharing Circles are loosely structured, and participants are expected to adhere to rules that promote the goals of the circle while assuring cooperation, effective communication, trust, and confidentiality.

Character develops within a social environment. The nature of the Sharing Circle environment — the messages it sends to students and the behaviors it encourages and discourages are highly conducive to character development. Students follow clear rules of conduct, accept ownership of those rules, are supportive of one another, and experience a sense of satisfaction by complying with the guidelines and procedures of the circle. Regular implementation of Sharing Circles can noticeably accelerate the development and internalization of the moral values addressed in this book.

Two Initial Pointers

To prepare yourself to take full advantage of the Sharing Circle process, thoroughly read and digest the portions of this section that deal with the Sharing Circle rules and procedures. As you are reading, keep two points in mind:

First, the topic elaborations provided under the heading, "Introduce the Topic," are guides for you to follow when presenting the topic to your students. They are excellent models, but need not be read verbatim. The idea is to focus the attention of students on the specific topic to be discussed. In your elaboration, try to use language and examples that are appropriate to the age, ability, and culture of your students.

Second, we strongly urge you to respect the integrity of the sharing and discussion phases of the circle. These two phases are procedurally and qualitatively different, yet of equal importance in promoting awareness, insight, and higher-level thinking in students. After you have led several circles, you will appreciate the instructional advantage of maintaining this unique relationship.

All Sharing Circle topics are intended to develop awareness and insight through voluntary sharing. This occurs in the first (or sharing) phase of the circle. The discussion phase of the circle, for which specific questions are provided, allows students to understand what has been shared at deeper levels, to evaluate ideas that have been generated by the topic, and to apply specific concepts to other areas of learning.

Helping Students Develop Moral Awareness

As students follow the rules and relate to each other verbally during the Sharing Circle, they are practicing respectful listening and oral communication. Through insights gained in the course of pondering and discussing the various topics, students become more aware of what constitutes good character as well as the need to develop control of their feelings, thoughts, and behaviors. Through the positive experience of give and take, they also learn the importance of interacting responsibly and effectively.

The Sharing Circle topics offered in this book address both moral values and important skills — keeping agreements, developing responsible habits, solving problems, demonstrating respect for self and others, being loyal, being trustworthy and honest, following rules, demonstrating kindness and consideration, resolving conflicts, etc.

Topics like these not only help students identify specific values, they provide a venue within which students can liberally use the "language of character," and they require students to describe incidents and behaviors from their own experience that illustrate those values.

The Sharing Circle allows students to confront difficult decision-making situations. In response to the topics posed, students are asked to state positions, to think about their reasons for selecting those positions, and to listen to the positions and reasoning of others.

Learning Right from Wrong

As students learn to relate effectively to others, moral issues surface again and again. Students learn that all people have the power to influence one another. They become aware not only of how others affect them, but of the effects their behaviors have on others.

The Sharing Circle process has been designed so that healthy, responsible behaviors are modeled by the teacher or counselor in his/her role as circle leader. Also, the rules require that the students relate responsibly and effectively to one another. The Sharing Circle brings out and affirms the positive qualities inherent in everyone and allows students to practice effective modes of communication. Because Sharing Circles provide a place where participants are listened to and their feelings accepted, students learn how to provide the same conditions to peers and adults outside the circle.

The Sharing Circle teaches cooperation. As equitably as possible, the circle structure attempts to meet the needs of all participants. Everyone's feelings are accepted; everyone's contributions are judged valuable. The circle is not another competitive arena, but is guided by a spirit of collaboration. When students practice fair, respectful interaction with one another, they benefit from the experience and are likely to employ these responsible behaviors in other life situations.

Practicing Responsible Behaviors

One of the great benefits of the Sharing Circle is that it does not merely teach young people about social interaction, it lets them interact! Every Sharing Circle is a real-life experience of social interaction where the students share, listen, explore, plan, and problem solve together. As they interact, they learn about each other and they realize what it takes to relate effectively to others. Any given Sharing Circle may provide a dozen tiny flashes of positive interpersonal insight for an individual participant. Gradually, the reality of what constitutes effective behavior in relating to others is internalized.

Through this sharing of interpersonal experiences, students learn that behavior can be positive or negative, and sometimes both at the same time. Consequences can be constructive, destructive, or both. Different people respond differently to the same event. They have different feelings and thoughts. The students begin to understand what will cause what to happen; they grasp the concept of cause and effect; they see themselves affecting others and being affected *by* others.

The ability to make accurate interpretations and responses in social situations allows students to know where they stand with themselves and with others. They can tell what actions "fit" a situation. Sharing Circles are marvelous testing grounds where students can observe themselves and others in action, and can begin to see themselves as contributing to the good and bad feelings of others. With this understanding, students are helped to conclude that being responsible towards others feels good, and is the most valuable and personally rewarding form of interaction.

How to Set Up Sharing Circles

Group Size and Composition. Sharing Circles are a time for focusing on individuals' contributions in an unhurried fashion. For this reason, each circle session group needs to be kept relatively small—eight to twelve usually works best. Once they move beyond the primary grades, students are capable of extensive verbalization. You will want to encourage this, and not stifle them because of time constraints.

Each group should be as heterogeneous as possible with respect to sex, ability, and racial/ethnic background. Sometimes there will be a group in which all the students are particularly reticent to speak. At these times, bring in an expressive student or two who will get things going. Sometimes it is necessary for practical reasons to change the membership of a group. Once established, however, it is advisable to keep a group as stable as possible.

Length and Location of Sharing Circles. Most circle sessions last approximately 10 to 20 minutes. At first students tend to be reluctant to express themselves fully because they do not yet know that the circle is a safe place. Consequently your first sessions may not last more than 10 to 15 minutes. Generally speaking, students become comfortable and motivated to speak with continued experience.

In middle-school classrooms circle sessions may be conducted at any time during the class period. Starting circle sessions at the beginning of the period allows additional time in case students become deeply involved in the topic. If you start circles late in the period, make sure the students are aware of their responsibility to be concise.

In elementary classes, any time of day is appropriate for Sharing Circles. Some teachers like to set the tone for the day by beginning with circles; others feel it's a perfect way to complete the day and to send the children away with positive feelings.

Circle sessions may be carried out wherever there is room for students to sit in a circle and experience few or no distractions. Most leaders prefer to have students sit in chairs rather than on the floor. Students seem to be less apt to invade one another's space while seated in chairs. Some leaders conduct sessions outdoors, with students seated in a secluded, grassy area.

How to Get Started

Teachers and counselors have used numerous methods to involve students in the circle process. What works well for one leader or class does not always work for another. Here are two basic strategies leaders have successfully used to get groups started. Whichever you use, we recommend that you post a chart listing the circle session rules and procedures to which every participant may refer.

1. Start one group at a time, and cycle through all groups. If possible, provide an opportunity for every student to experience a circle session in a setting where there are no disturbances. This may mean arranging for another staff member or aide to take charge of the students not participating in the circle. Non-participants may work on course work or silent reading, or, if you have a cooperative librarian, they may be sent to the library to work independently or in small groups on a class assignment. Repeat this procedure until all of the students have been involved in at least one circle session.

Next, initiate a class discussion about the circle sessions. Explain that from now on you will be meeting with each circle group in the classroom, with the remainder of the class present. Ask the students to help you plan established procedures for the remainder of the class to follow.

Meet with each circle session group on a different day, systematically cycling through the groups.

2. Combine inner and outer circles. Meet with one circle session group while another group listens and observes as an outer circle. Then have the two groups change places, with the students on the outside becoming the inner circle, and responding verbally to the topic. If you run out of time in middle-school classrooms, use two class periods for this. Later, a third group may be added to this alternating cycle. The end product of this arrangement is two or more groups (comprising everyone in the class) meeting together simultaneously. While one group is involved in discussion, the other groups listen and observe as members of an outer circle. If you like, invite the members of the outer circle to participate in the review and discussion phases of the circle.

What To Do With the Rest of the Class

A number of arrangements can be made for students who are not participating in circle sessions. Here are some ideas:

- Arrange the room to ensure privacy. This may involve placing a circle of chairs or carpeting in a corner, away from other work areas. You might construct dividers from existing furniture, such as bookshelves or screens, or simply arrange chairs and tables in such a way that the circle area is protected from distractions.

- Involve aides, counselors, parents, or fellow teachers. Have an aide conduct a lesson with the rest of the class while you meet with a circle group. If you do not have an aide assigned to you, use auxiliary staff or parent volunteers.

- Have students work quietly on subject-area assignments in pairs or small, task-oriented groups.

- Utilize student aides or leaders. If the seat-work activity is in a content area, appoint students who show ability in that area as "consultants," and have them assist other students.

- Give the students plenty to do. List academic activities on the board. Make materials for quiet individual activities available so that students cannot run out of things to do and be tempted to consult you or disturb others.

- Make the activity of students outside the circle enjoyable. When you can involve the rest of the class in something meaningful to them, students will probably be less likely to interrupt the circle.

- Have the students work on an ongoing project. When they have a task in progress, students can simply resume where they left off, with little or no introduction from you. In these cases, appointing a "person in charge," "group leader," or "consultant" is wise.

- Allow individual journal-writing. While a circle is in progress, have the other students make entries in a private (or share-with-teacher-only) journal. The topic for journal writing could be the same topic that is being discussed in the Sharing Circle. Do not correct the journals, but if you read them, be sure to respond to the entries with your own written thoughts, where appropriate.

Leading the Sharing Circle

This section is a thorough guide for conducting Sharing Circles. It covers major points to keep in mind and answers questions which will arise as you begin using the program. Please remember that these guidelines are presented to assist you, not to restrict you. Follow them and trust your own leadership style at the same time.

Sharing Circle Procedures for the Leader

1. Setting up the circle
   (1-2 minutes)

2. Reviewing the ground rules
   (1-2 minutes) *

3. Introducing the topic
   (1-2 minutes)

4. Sharing by circle members
   (5-8 minutes)

5. Reviewing what is shared
   (3-5 minutes) **

6. Summary discussion
   (2-6 minutes)

7. Closing the circle
   (less than 1 minute)

*optional after the first few sessions
**optional

Setting up the circle (1-2 minutes)

As you sit down with the students in the circle, remember that you are not teaching a lesson. You are facilitating a group of people. Establish a positive atmosphere. In a relaxed manner, address each student by name, using eye contact and conveying warmth. An attitude of seriousness blended with enthusiasm will let the students know that the circle session is an important learning experience—an activity that can be interesting and meaningful.

Reviewing the ground rules (1-2 minutes)

At the beginning of the first session, and at appropriate intervals thereafter, go over the rules for the circle session. They are:

Sharing Circle Rules

1. Bring yourself to the circle and nothing else.

2. Everyone gets a turn to share, including the leader.

3. You can skip your turn if you wish.

4. Listen to the person who is sharing.

5. The time is shared equally.

6. Stay in your own space.

7. There are no interruptions, probing, put-downs, or gossip.

From this point on, demonstrate to the students that you expect them to remember and abide by the ground rules. Convey that you think well of them and know they are fully capable of responsible behavior. Let them know that by coming to the session they are making a commitment to listen and show acceptance and respect for the other students and you.

Introducing the topic (1-2 minutes)

State the topic in your own words. Elaborate and provide examples as each activity suggests. Add clarifying statements of your own that will help the students understand the topic. Answer questions about the topic, and emphasize that there are no "right" responses. Finally, restate the topic, opening the session to responses (theirs and yours). Sometimes taking your turn first helps the students understand the aim of the topic. At various points throughout the session, state the topic again.

Just prior to leading a circle session, contemplate the topic and think of at least one possible response that you can make to it.

Sharing by circle members (12-18 minutes)

The most important point to remember is this: The purpose of the circle session is to give students an opportunity to express themselves and be accepted for the experiences, thoughts, and feelings they share. Avoid taking the action away from the circle members. They are the stars!

Reviewing what is shared (optional 3-5 minutes)

Besides modeling effective listening (the very best way to teach it) and positively reinforcing students for attentive listening, a review can be used to deliberately improve listening skills in circle members.

Reviewing is a time for reflective listening, when circle members feed back what they heard each other say during the sharing phase of the circle. Besides encouraging effective listening, reviewing provides circle members with additional recognition. It validates their experience and conveys the idea, "you are important," a message we can all profit from hearing often.

To review, a circle member simply addresses someone who shared, and briefly paraphrases what the person said ("John, I heard you say....").

The first few times you conduct reviews, stress the importance of checking with the speaker to see if the review accurately summarized the main things that were shared. If the speaker says, "No," allow him or her to make corrections. Stress too, the importance of speaking directly to the speaker, using the person's name and the pronoun "you," not "he" or "she." If someone says, "She said that...," intervene as promptly and respectfully as possible and say to the reviewer, "Talk to Betty...Say you." This is very important. The person whose turn is being reviewed will have a totally different feeling when talked to, instead of about.

Note: Remember that the review is optional and is most effective when used occasionally, not as a part of every circle.

Summary discussion (2-8 minutes)

The summary discussion is the cognitive portion of the circle session. During this phase, the leader asks thought-provoking questions to stimulate free discussion and higher-level thinking. Each circle session in this book includes several summary questions. Choose from these, but ask no more than one or two. Asking too many questions shifts the emphasis of the circle from sharing to discussion, a consequence that should be avoided. At times you may want to formulate questions that are more appropriate to the level of understanding in your group—or to what was actually shared in the circle. If you wish to make connections between the circle session topic and your content area, ask questions that will accomplish that objective and allow the summary discussion to extend longer.

It is important that you not confuse the summary with the review. The review is optional; the summary is not. The summary meets the need of people of all ages to find meaning in what they do. Thus, the summary serves as a necessary culmination to each circle session by allowing the students to clarify the key concepts they gained from the session.

Closing the circle (less than 1 minute)

The ideal time to end a circle session is when the summary discussion reaches natural closure. Sincerely thank everyone for being part of the circle. Don't thank specific students for speaking, as doing so might convey the impression that speaking is more appreciated than mere listening. Then close the circle by saying, "The circle session is over," or "OK, that ends our session."

More about Sharing Circle Procedures and Rules

The next few paragraphs offer further clarification concerning circle session leadership.

Why should students bring themselves to the circle and nothing else? Individual teachers differ on this point, but most prefer that students not bring objects (such as pencils, books, etc.) to the circle that may be distracting.

Who gets to talk? Everyone. The importance of acceptance in Sharing Circles cannot be overly stressed. In one way or another practically every ground rule says one thing: accept one another. When you model acceptance of students, they will learn how to be accepting. Each individual in the circle is important and deserves a turn to speak if he or she wishes to take it. Equal opportunity to become involved should be given to everyone in the circle.

Circle members should be reinforced equally for their contributions. There are many reasons why a leader may become more enthused over what one student shares than another. The response may be more on target, reflect more depth, be more entertaining, be philosophically more in keeping with one's own point of view, and so on. However, students need to be given equal recognition for their contributions, even if the contribution is to listen silently throughout the session.

In most of the circle sessions, plan to take a turn and address the topic, too. Students usually appreciate it very much and learn a great deal when their teachers and counselors are willing to tell about their own experiences, thoughts, and feelings. In this way you let your students know that you acknowledge your own humanness.

Does everyone have to take a turn?
No. Students may choose to skip their turns. If the circle becomes a pressure situation in which the members are coerced in any way to speak, it will become an unsafe place where participants are not comfortable. Meaningful discussion is unlikely in such an atmosphere. By allowing students to make this choice, you are showing them that you accept their right to remain silent if that is what they choose to do.

As you begin circles, it will be to your advantage if one or more students decline to speak. If you are imperturbable and accepting when this happens, you let them know you are offering them an opportunity to experience something you think is valuable, or at least worth a try, and not attempting to force-feed them. You as a leader should not feel compelled to share a personal experience in every session, either. However, if you decline to speak in most of the sessions, this may have an inhibiting effect on the students' willingness to share.

A word should also be said about how this ground rule has sometimes been carried to extremes. Sometimes leaders have bent over backwards to let students know they don't have to take a turn. This seeming lack of enthusiasm on the part of the leader has caused reticence in the students. In order to avoid this outcome, don't project any personal insecurity as you lead the session. Be confident in your proven ability to work with students. Expect something to happen and it will.

Some circle leaders ask the participants to raise their hands when they wish to speak, while others simply allow free verbal sharing without soliciting the leader's permission first. Choose the procedure that works best for you, but do not call on anyone unless you can see signs of readiness. And do not merely go around the circle.

Some leaders have reported that their first circles fell flat—that no one, or just one or two students, had anything to say. But they continued to have circles, and at a certain point everything changed. Thereafter, the students had a great deal to say that these leaders considered worth waiting for. It appears that in these cases the leaders' acceptance of the right to skip turns was a key factor. In time most students will contribute verbally when they have something they want to say, and when they are assured there is no pressure to do so.

Sometimes a silence occurs during a circle session. Don't feel you have to jump in every time someone stops talking. During silences students have an opportunity to think about what they would like to share or to contemplate an important idea they've heard. A general rule of thumb is to allow silence to the point that you observe group discomfort. At that point move on. Do not switch to another topic. To do so implies you will not be satisfied until the students speak. If you change to another topic, you are telling them you didn't really mean it when you said they didn't have to take a turn if they didn't want to.

If you are bothered about students who attend a number of circles and still do not share verbally, reevaluate what you consider to be involvement. Participation does not necessarily mean talking. Students who do not speak are listening and learning.

How can I encourage effective listening? The Sharing Circle is a time (and place) for students and leaders to strengthen the habit of listening by doing it over and over again. No one was born knowing how to listen effectively to others. It is a skill like any other that gets better as it is practiced. In the immediacy of the circle session, the members become keenly aware of the necessity to listen, and most students respond by expecting it of one another.

In the Sharing Circle, listening is defined as the respectful focusing of attention on individual speakers. It includes eye contact with the speaker and open body posture. It eschews interruptions of any kind. When you conduct a circle session, listen and encourage listening in the students by (1) focusing your attention on the person who is speaking, (2) being receptive to what the speaker is saying (not mentally planning your next remark), and (3) recognizing the speaker when she finishes speaking, either verbally ("Thanks, Shirley") or nonverbally (a nod and a smile).

To encourage effective listening in the students, reinforce them by letting them know you have noticed they were listening to each other and you appreciate it. Occasionally conducting a review after the sharing phase also has the effect of sharpening listening skills.

How can I ensure the students get equal time? When circle members share the time equally, they demonstrate their acceptance of the notion that everyone's contribution is of equal importance. It is not uncommon to have at least one dominator in a group. This person is usually totally unaware that by continuing to talk he or she is taking time from others who are less assertive.

Be very clear with the students about the purpose of this ground rule. Tell them at the outset how much time there is and whether or not you plan to conduct a review. When it is your turn, always limit your own contribution. If someone goes on and on, do intervene (dominators need to know what they are doing), but do so as gently and respectfully as you can.

What are some examples of put-downs? Put-downs convey the message, "You are not okay as you are." Some put-downs are deliberate, but many are made unknowingly. Both kinds are undesirable in a Sharing Circle because they destroy the atmosphere of acceptance and disrupt the flow of discussion. Typical put-downs include:

- overquestioning.
- statements that have the effect of teaching or preaching
- advice giving
- one-upsmanship
- criticism, disapproval, or objections
- sarcasm
- statements or questions of disbelief

How can I deal with put-downs?
There are two major ways for dealing with put-downs in circle sessions: preventing them from occurring and intervening when they do.

Going over the ground rules with the students at the beginning of each session, particularly in the earliest sessions, is a helpful preventive technique. Another is to reinforce the students when they adhere to the rule. Be sure to use nonpatronizing, nonevaluative language.

Unacceptable behavior should be stopped the moment it is recognized by the leader. When you become aware that a put-down is occurring, do whatever you ordinarily do to stop destructive behavior in the classroom. If one student gives another an unasked-for bit of advice, say for example, "Jane, please give Alicia a chance to tell her story." To a student who interrupts say, "Ed, it's Sally's turn." In most cases the fewer words, the better—students automatically tune out messages delivered as lectures.

Sometimes students disrupt the group by starting a private conversation with the person next to them. Touch the offender on the arm or shoulder while continuing to give eye contact to the student who is speaking. If you can't reach the offender, simply remind him or her of the rule about listening. If students persist in putting others down during circle sessions, ask to see them at another time and hold a brief one-to-one conference, urging them to follow the rules. Suggest that they reconsider their membership in the circle. Make it clear that if they don't intend to honor the ground rules, they are not to come to the circle.

How can I keep students from gossiping? Periodically remind students that using names and sharing embarrassing information is not acceptable. Urge the students to relate personally to one another, but not to tell intimate details of their lives.

What should the leader do during the summary discussion? Conduct the summary as an open forum, giving students the opportunity to discuss a variety of ideas and accept those that make sense to them. Don't impose your opinions on the students, or allow the students to impose theirs on one another. Ask open-ended questions, encourage higher-level thinking, contribute your own ideas when appropriate, and act as a facilitator.

Trustworthiness

The activities in this section deal with four components of trustworthiness: *Honesty, Integrity, Promise-keeping*, and *Loyalty*. To be worthy of trust, students need to understand these values and behave in accordance with them. When *you* care deeply about the same values — naming, discussing, modeling, and supporting them consistently —much of the teaching will already be done. Here are some guidelines:

Honesty. Give students honest answers. If you don't know or aren't sure, admit it. If you don't think it is appropriate to talk about a subject or if you must withhold information for some reason, say so and explain why. Expect students to tell the truth and do their own work. Don't tolerate cheating, trickery, or deviousness.

Integrity. Demonstrate your beliefs through your behavior. Stand up for what you think is right and speak out about what you think is wrong. Model commitment and courage. Help students verbalize their beliefs by creating an ongoing forum on values.

Promise-keeping. Keep your word. Return homework and test papers on time. If you promise to seek out a piece of information or locate and read a particular book, do it. Likewise, follow though on suggested field trips and special activities, even if the logistics prove difficult. Expect students to complete their work on time, return borrowed items in good condition, and keep their commitments.

Loyalty. Show your support for everyone in the school community. Don't gossip about or criticize students, colleagues, or parents behind their backs. Never participate in rumor mongering. Attempt to stop the spread of rumors and gossip among students as soon as you become aware of them. When students are protective and supportive of one another, point out that they are being loyal and are thereby earning trust.

What Does It Mean to Be Trustworthy?
Brainstorming an Action Plan

Purpose:
To explore the components of trustworthiness and brainstorm ways in which those components can be demonstrated in the classroom, school, home, neighborhood, and nation.

Materials:
paper and pencils; chalkboard or whiteboard and writing implements

Procedure:
Write the word *trustworthiness* in large letters on the board. Ask the students if anyone knows what trustworthiness means. Invite volunteers to share their ideas. Incorporating any definitions the students offer, explain that trustworthiness means to be worthy, or deserving, of someone's trust or confidence. If you are trustworthy, people can count on you. You can be depended upon to keep your promises, to be honest, to do what you know is right, and to be loyal to those who trust you.

Tell the students that there are four components of trustworthiness: *honesty*, *integrity*, *promise-keeping*, and *loyalty*. In your own words, give a brief description of each. For example, you might say:

Honesty is accomplishing or earning something fairly, without cheating or stealing. It also means telling the truth. Integrity is being true to your beliefs, or living by your values. In other words, integrity is doing what you believe to be right. Promise-keeping is just like it sounds — keeping your promises and agreements. Loyalty is being true to those who trust you and depend on you. For example, a loyal friend is willing to say and do things for you publicly. A loyal American publicly stands up for or defends this country and its government.

Divide the class into eight groups of three or four. Assign one component of trustworthiness to each group, making sure that every component is assigned twice. In other words, two groups will be working on honesty, two on integrity, two on promise-keeping, and two on loyalty.

Distribute writing materials, and ask the groups to brainstorm ways in which their component of trustworthiness can be demonstrated in the school, home, neighborhood (or community), and nation. Have them write an action plan which explains how their component can be carried out and supported in each of those places. Write the following sentence pattern on the board for the groups to copy and complete, using their ideas. Instruct the groups to complete the sentence four times, once for each location (school, home, neighborhood, nation).

> **We can demonstrate** _____ **in the**
> _____(name of component)_____
> _____**by** _____.
> (school, home, neighborhood or nation)   (behaviors that support the concept)

When the students are finished brainstorming, ask the groups with the same component to meet briefly and share their ideas. Next, gather the whole class together for sharing. Make a chart on the board, listing the words **Honesty**, **Integrity**, **Promise-keeping**, and **Loyalty** in a column along the left side. Draw horizontal lines under each word and extend the lines across the board. Across the top of the chart, write **School**, **Home**, **Neighborhood**, and **Nation**. Draw vertical lines to separate the locations, extending the lines down to complete the grid. As the groups share their ideas, invite them to fill in their portion of the chart.

Tell the students that it is now time to develop and implement a *personal* action plan. Have the students each choose one component that they would be willing to practice for two weeks. Have them write their action plan for the selected component on a clean sheet of paper, using the same sentence pattern that the groups used. Ask the students to keep a daily journal describing specific things they did to support their action plan. Remind them to explain how the component was supported by each behavior. Share journal entries at the end of the two weeks. Conclude the activity with a summary discussion.

Discussion Questions:
1. What difficulties did you have carrying out your action plan? What was easiest about it?
2. What would life be like if no one demonstrated the components of trustworthiness?
3. What did you learn about your own behavior from this activity?

Adaptation:
Primary children may find it extremely difficult to understand and discuss all four components. If you believe this is the case with your students, discuss only the components of honesty and promise-keeping, concepts which young children can understand. Have the class brainstorm behaviors while you record them. Limit the locations to school and home. Have the entire class focus on one concept each week and keep a class log of supporting behaviors.

	School	Home	Neighborhood	Nation
Honesty				
Integrity				
Promise-keeping				
Loyalty				

The Value of Loyalty
Video, Writing, and Art

Purpose:
By analyzing the loyalty exhibited by a dog for its master, the students develop a definition of loyalty, and then explore ways in which they can be loyal to family, friends, community, and nation.

Materials:
Videotape of a classic "dog story" ("Lassie," "Homeward Bound," "Old Yeller," or "Call of the Wild"), VCR and monitor; chalkboard or whiteboard and writing implements; student writing materials; pictures of dogs, construction paper in several colors, scissors, glue, and colored markers.

Procedure:
Show the video. When it is over, ask the students questions to help them focus on the values portrayed in the film. The following questions are general and should be adapted to specifically address the film you show:
— *What was the relationship between the dog in this story and its master?*
— *What did the dog do to prove its loyalty?*
— *What did the dog's master do to earn that loyalty?*
— *What were the master's feelings toward the dog?*
— *What feelings did you experience watching the movie, and why?*

Discuss the loyalty of the dog against all odds and in difficult circumstances. Explain that it is in the nature of dogs to obey their masters. A dog often becomes so attached to a master that it will defend and protect the person from perceived danger. Dogs such as Lassie and Old Yeller are *loyal*. Loyal means faithful.

Use the example of the canine hero to apply the concept of loyalty to people. Explain that people can also be loyal (or faithful) to friends, family, community, country, or groups to which they belong (such as a baseball team or cooperative group). The "Pledge of Allegiance" is a promise of loyalty to the nation. When you recite the pledge, you are promising to be true to the United States and to protect and preserve it.

Make a word web on the chalkboard. Print the heading "Loyalty" in the middle of the board and draw an oval around it. Then draw several straight lines radiating outward from the edge of the oval. At the end of each line, write the name of a category or group to which a person can be loyal — e.g., family, friends, school, team, cooperative group, community, nation.

Divide the students into groups of three or four and explain the task:

Working together, think of at least one way in which you can show loyalty in each of the categories on the board and write it down on paper. For example, to show loyalty to friends, you might write, "Be nice to friends and don't say bad things about them." To show loyalty to the community, you might write, "Obey the law and report any crime you see."

After the groups have written one or more ideas for each category, have them report to the class.

Announce that the students will now have an opportunity to write one idea about demonstrating loyalty on the silhouette of a dog made from construction paper. Show the students pictures of dogs from books, magazines, or posters. In your own words, explain:

Choose a dog shape, and draw a large outline of the shape on a piece of construction paper. Cut out the dog and glue it to a second piece of construction paper, creating a silhouette. To make the silhouette stand out, choose a contrasting color for the background. With a colored marker (or chalk if the dog silhouette is black), write a loyalty statement of your own directly on the silhouette of the dog.

Circulate and assist, making sure that each of the categories on the board is represented in the work of at least one student. When the students have completed the art assignment, invite them to share their statements with the class. Post the pictures on a bulletin board entitled, "Dogs Show Us the Value of Loyalty."

Ask questions to stimulate a summary discussion and to encourage further thinking:

Discussion Questions:
1. Why is it important to be loyal to your friends (family, team, community, nation)?
2. How would you feel if a friend were disloyal to you? What would you do?
3. Do you have a right to expect loyalty from a friend no matter what you do? What if you do something illegal or dangerous?
4. What do you have to do to earn a person's loyalty?

Variations:
Instead of showing the video, read the book from which the suggested movie was adapted (or allow the students to read one of several books). Extend the activity over 2 to 3 weeks.

Obtain a copy of the words and music to "Old Dog Tray" by Stephen Foster. Sing it with your class or read it as a poem. The chorus goes like this:

Old Dog Tray is ever faithful.
Grief cannot drive him away.
He is gentle. He is kind.
I'll never, never find
A better dog than Old Dog Tray.
　　　　　　　　　—Stephen Foster

Lies, Lies, Lies
Dramatizing a Story

Purpose:
This activity uses stories and dramatizations to help students experience and understand consequences (including feelings) that result from lying.

Materials:
Books with passages in which someone lies and feels guilty or suffers consequences (*Otherwise Known As Sheila the Great*, by Judy Blume; *A Big, Fat, Enormous Lie* by Marjorie Sharmat; *Petunia* by Roger Duvoisin).

Procedure:
Tell a story like the one below, or read a passage from a book in which someone lies and gets caught or feels badly.

The Big Lie

Suzie sat excitedly at breakfast. She couldn't eat fast enough. Neither could her mom and the aunts and uncles she was visiting for the summer. There was a big fair in town and, today, they were all going to attend it. In her mind Suzie could already see the clowns, feel the thrill of the rides, smell the cotton candy and popcorn, and hear the barkers crying, "Knock over just three ducks and win a fabulous toy," or "Step right up and let me guess your weight." When the family was finally ready, Suzie's mom said to her, "You may choose one present for yourself at the fair and I will buy it for you." Suzie couldn't wait to see all of the displays of toys so she could make her choice.

At the fair, Suzie was dazzled by so many beautiful things. As she strolled in front of the booths, she narrowed her choices to a beautiful heart-shaped ring and a soft, cuddly teddy bear. Oh, what a difficult choice! Suzie really wanted them both. At last Suzie told her mom that she wanted the ring, so her mom bought it for her. As they walked around other parts of the fair, Suzie admired the ring on her finger, but she kept thinking of the teddy bear. Then she had an idea. Without anyone noticing, Suzie slipped the ring in her pocket.

Just before stopping for lunch, Suzie cried, "I've lost my ring!" All the family looked around on the ground, but the ring was gone. Suzie's mother felt so sorry for her that she offered to buy her another one. Suzie sniffled, "No, I want the teddy bear." So her mom took her to the booth with the teddy bear and bought it for her. Suzie was delighted that she had fooled her mom and family, and had both presents.

When Suzie sat down for lunch with her family, she reached in her pocket to check if her ring was still there. Satisfied that the ring was safe, she pulled out her hand. However, the ring accidently came out with her hand and fell on the ground. When the family saw the ring drop to the ground, they knew what Suzie had been up to. They knew that she lied about the lost ring. "You lied to us," her aunt said severely. "How could you have done such a thing?" her mom said as she stared at Suzie in disbelief. "What a bad girl you are!" an uncle scolded.

For the rest of the day, the family acted very cool toward Suzie. She felt awful. She wished she hadn't lied. Her behavior ruined the day for her and her family. Suzie vowed to herself that she would never lie again, no matter how difficult it might be.

Ask the students to help you sequence the events in the story. Create additional dialogue by talking about what Suzie and the other characters might have said in each scene and why. Next, ask for volunteers to act out the story.

After the first group of students has dramatized the story, ask a second group to role-play the same story. Explain to the actors:

We're going to do this role play a little differently. Sometime during each scene, I will say, "Freeze." When you hear that word, hold your positions and stop talking. I will walk among you and tap different actors on the shoulder. When you feel a tap, tell us what your character is thinking and feeling at that moment. I may tap just one person, or I may tap several during each of these "freeze" periods. Continue with the role play when you hear me say, "Resume."

Have several groups of volunteers act out "The Big Lie." Follow the same procedure with other stories as well. Read passages from books (see above) in which a character tells a lie and feels badly about lying and/or gets caught in a lie. Allow one group to act out the sequence of events uninterrupted before adding the "freeze-resume" technique. Conclude the activity with a summary discussion.

Discussion Questions:

1. How do you feel when you know that someone has lied to you?
2. If you frequently lied about yourself and your accomplishments, how do you think other people would react if they found out?
3. Do you think that lying can become a habit — something a person does without thinking? If so, how can that habit be changed?
4. Why should we make truthfulness a habit?

Cheating Hurts
Discussion and Poster Making

Purpose:
To examine the consequences of cheating and to express new understandings through art.

Materials:
large pieces of butcher paper; drawing paper, art supplies, and writing implements

Procedure:
Begin by asking the students: *Do you know what cheating is?*

Discuss the meaning of cheating, inviting the students to share their perceptions. Add to their ideas by explaining that cheating is getting something in a dishonest way. Ask the students to think of some examples of cheating in school. List their suggestions on the board, adding ideas of your own. The list should include:
— copying answers from someone else's paper instead of doing your own work.
— erasing someone's name from a paper and putting your own name on it.
— taking the teacher's answer book and getting answers to an assignment.
— getting someone else to do your work for you.

Have the students form groups of three or four. Explain that their task is to brainstorm as many reasons as they can think of why cheating is wrong. Have them focus on the possible effects, or consequences, of cheating in school.

Give each group a sheet of butcher paper and a colored marker. Ask them to select a scribe to record their ideas in large lettering on the butcher paper. Allow 5 to 10 minutes to complete the task. When time is up, ask one member from each group to report to the whole class. Post the lists around the room.

If the following "reasons why cheating is wrong" are not included on the student lists, discuss them with the students while recording them on a separate list of your own. Post this list also.
- You lose the teacher's trust that you will do your own work.
- If you cheat in school, you may find it easier to cheat outside of school.
- You will lose your self-respect and pride.
- Cheating is a lie because it causes people to think you know more than you do.
- Cheating may lead to other forms of lying.
- Cheating is not fair to students who are honest.
- If you get into the habit of cheating when you are young, you will find it easier to cheat when you are older.
- Cheating is taking something that you haven't earned, and may lead to other forms of stealing.

Announce that the students are going to have an opportunity to express one of their ideas about cheating in poster form. Distribute the art materials. Suggest that the students choose one "reason why cheating is wrong" from a posted list and try to express that idea in as few words as possible, combining the words with a picture or symbol to complete the poster. For example, the words might read:

✔ **Choose to Cheat? Lose Self-Respect!**

✔ **Cheating is Lying**

✔ **Cheating: Unfair to Others!**

✔ **Cheat in School? Cheat Out of School!**

✔ **Young Cheaters Become Old Cheaters**

When the posters are finished, invite the students to share them with the class. Then display the posters on a bulletin board in the school auditorium or library under the heading, "Cheating Is Wrong Because..."

Conclude the activity with discussion.

Discussion Questions:
1. How would you feel if someone cheated on a test and got a better score than you?
2. How would you feel if someone took your work and put his/her name on it?
3. How does cheating hurt the community? ...the country? ...the world?
4. How does cheating hurt the cheater?

Variation:
In primary classrooms, allow the children to brainstorm their ideas while you record them on the board. Write a list of five or six short phrases for the children to choose from when making their posters.

Can You Be Trusted?
Guided Exploration and Discussion

Purpose:
By making agreements and fulfilling them, the students experience, and then analyze, factors involved in trust-building.

Materials:
a safe grassy area, such as a playground or park, that is secure from hazards and open enough to provide good visibility (for you)

> **Caution:** Choose a safe environment where you can see all students at all times. If an appropriate outdoor area is not available, move furniture and equipment out of the way and conduct the activity indoors, limiting the number of partners on the floor at any one time.

Procedure:
Begin this activity by discussing the meaning of trust. Ask the students what it means to "trust another person" or "be in someone's trust." Make sure you cover the following concepts:
—depending on
—relying on
—putting yourself in someone else's hands
—having confidence in
—keeping agreements
—expecting an outcome (trusting that an expected outcome will occur)

Ask volunteers to share examples showing how people put their trust in others, *e.g.*, children depend on parents to provide them with enough to eat and a safe home; a parent trusts an older child to watch a younger sibling while the parent is making dinner.

Explain to the students that they are going to participate in a two-part activity in which partners work together to build trust. In your own words, give these instructions:

One of you will close his or her eyes, pretending to be sightless, and the other will guide the sightless person around the playground. When you are the guide, you must make two or three agreements with your partner before beginning the walk. These can be promises concerning safety, speed, kinds of movement you will be performing, or warnings about approaching changes in terrain. For example, you might state, "I agree to warn you when we are about to go up hill or down, or when I want you to slow down. I also agree to tell you what you will be touching before you touch it." Another example might be, "I promise not to make you walk into any holes, touch anything dirty like someone's old garbage, or make you bump into anything." As a guide, you must lead your partner around the area safely, while providing opportunities for your partner to touch different objects, listen to sounds, and smell various aromas. You are to be very careful and must never lead your partner into anything that might be dangerous. You may talk to each other during the walk.

Ask the students to choose a partner or assign pairs, as necessary. Allow 5 to 10 minutes for the walk. When the time is up, blow a whistle or otherwise signal the partners to return to a central location. Direct them to change roles, and have the new guides make their agreements before starting the second walk.

After both walks are completed, bring the group together and debrief the two walks.

Discussion Questions:
1. What were some of your experiences while you were either the blindfolded person or the guide?
2. Did your guide live up to his/her agreements?
3. Did your guide's performance help build or break down trust?
4. How did you feel while depending upon another person?
5. If your guide hadn't fulfilled his/her responsibility, what might have happened?
6. What did you learn about trust from this activity?
7. How can we build trust with each other in class? ...in school? ...at home?

Variation:
Older students may enjoy another movement activity called the "Trust Circle." Have eight to ten students form a tight circle. Ask one person to stand stiffly in the middle with arms folded snugly across his/her chest. Then have one of the circle members reach out and hold the middle student by the shoulders while that student leans backwards. Finally, direct the circle members to pass the middle student around by the shoulders while his/her feet remain in center of the circle. Repeat the exercise, giving every student an opportunity to be in the middle. Be sure to monitor and control the activity carefully, ensuring the safe and respectful treatment of every student.

Character Report Card
Reading and Evaluating

Purpose:
To become aware of the elements of trustworthiness by examining the actions of book characters.

Materials:
narrative books, chalkboard or whiteboard and writing implements, and student writing materials

Note: This activity is best completed after the others in this unit, as it *reviews* the four elements of trustworthiness.

Procedure:
The day before this activity, ask the students to each bring one or two books that they have read or are nearly finished reading. Or, distribute picture books and allow the students time to read at least one.

Review the concept of trustworthiness and the four elements that comprise it: *honesty, integrity, promise-keeping,* and *loyalty.* (See the first activity in this unit.) Point out that these elements can be seen in the behavior of people in many situations. They can also be found in many stories. In some cases, the behavior of story characters suggests an absence of these elements.

Tell the students that they will have an opportunity to select one of the characters from their book and evaluate the character's behaviors by means of a report card. Create an example of a report card on the board, while explaining:

Design the report card, using "Honesty," "Integrity," "Promise-keeping," and "Loyalty" as subjects. You may use letter or number grades, but you must explain their meaning at the bottom of the report card. For example, "A" can mean excellent; "B," good; "C," fair; "D," poor; and "F, " failing. Make a grid with the words "Subject," "Grade," and "Comments" written across the top with vertical lines separating them. List the four subjects under the "Subjects" heading and separate them with horizontal lines. Write the character's name at the top of the report card as well as the name of the book from which the character was chosen.

For your example, select a character from a story that all of the students know, such as the wolf in "The Three Little Pigs." Ask the students to agree on a grade for each of the four subjects. Write the grade in the appropriate column on the board. Ask for a reason for the grade and write it under the "Comments" heading. For example, the students might give the wolf an "A" in honesty and explain in their comments: "He said he would blow the pigs' houses down if they didn't let him in, and he did. He even tried to blow down the house of bricks." The students might give him a "D" or "F" for loyalty, however. The "Comment" might be: "He was not loyal to the pigs as fellow members of the community."

Distribute writing materials and have the students design and create their own report cards. Remind them that a reason for each grade must be written under the "Comments" heading. When they are finished, invite the students to share their report cards with the whole group. Facilitate discussion at appropriate points during the sharing, and to summarize and conclude the activity.

Discussion Questions:
1. How can you tell if someone is trustworthy?
2. When a person is dishonest, how does that affect your willingness to trust the person?
3. Would you expect others to trust you if you were dishonest?
4. Why is it important to have trustworthy people as leaders? ...as friends?

Extension:
Complete this activity again at the end of all the units in this book, using the six major values (Trustworthiness, Respect, Responsibility, Caring, Citizenship, Justice and Fairness) as "subjects" on the report card.

A Time I Kept My Promise
A Sharing Circle

Purpose:
To encourage the value of keeping promises.

Introduce the Topic:
Today's topic is, "A Time I Kept My Promise." Have you ever made a promise to someone and kept it? You said that you were going to do something, or not do something, and you followed through — even though it might have taken some hard work. Maybe you promised your dad that you would sweep the kitchen or patio after school and you did it. Perhaps you made a promise to a friend that you would go to his house on a Saturday to help with math homework and you went, even though you had to give up a more enjoyable activity. Maybe you promised your teacher that you would try harder to be quiet during study time, and by really working at it you succeeded. How did you feel about keeping your word? Did anyone notice it or acknowledge you for keeping the promise? Was your promise a promise not to do something, like not to fight with your sister or brother when mom left you two alone? Try to remember a time that you made a promise and kept it, and get ready to share it with the group. The topic is, "A Time I Kept My Promise."

Summary Discussion Questions:
1. Why is it important to keep promises when we make them?
2. How does it feel when someone makes a promise to you and keeps it? ...doesn't keep it?
3. How does keeping, or not keeping, promises affect the willingness of others to trust you?

Topic Variations:
A Time Someone Made a Promise to Me and Kept It

A Time I Didn't Keep My Promise

A Promise That Was Hard to Keep

I Told the Truth and Was Glad
A Sharing Circle

Purpose:
To help students develop an awareness of the consequences of dishonesty, and to encourage truthfulness.

Introduce the Topic:
Today's topic is, "I Told the Truth and Was Glad." Do you remember a time when you told the truth and were happy that you did? Maybe you were going to lie because that would have been easier, but you decided to tell the truth. Perhaps you spilled something on the sofa, or broke something, and didn't tell anyone at first, but admitted that you did it when an adult asked. Did you feel relieved after being honest, even if it meant paying for your mistake in some way? Maybe you saw a classmate stealing money from someone's desk and when the teacher asked if anyone knew what happened to the money you told the truth. Or maybe after lying about something, you felt bad, so you admitted your lie and told the truth. Think of a time that you told the truth and were glad that you did, even if it was hard to do. The topic is, "I Told the Truth and Was Glad."

Summary Discussion Questions:
1. Why is it important to tell the truth even when it is difficult?
2. How do you feel about yourself when you lie? ...when you are truthful?
3. How will telling the truth now make your life better when you are an adult?

Topic Variations:
A Time I Lied and Felt Guilty

I Felt Bad When Someone Lied to Me

A Time Someone Trusted Me
A Sharing Circle

Purpose:
To challenge students to think about the consequences of being or not being trustworthy. To encourage the value of trustworthiness.

Introduce the Topic:
Today's topic is: "A Time Someone Trusted Me." All of us have been in situations that required someone to trust us. Usually in these situations, we are asked to do something, such as carrying out a task, or to refrain from doing something, such as telling a secret. Think of a time when someone trusted you. Perhaps your dad wanted to show you a surprise he bought for your mom but you had to promise not to tell. Or maybe a friend asked you to take care of his goldfish while he was on vacation. Maybe an adult trusted you to watch a younger child in the park. Or a teacher trusted you to return a borrowed book the next day. Did you do what you said you would do or did you let that person down? Did you earn the trust placed in you or did you prove untrustworthy? How did the other person react? How did you feel? Think of a time when someone trusted you and you either followed through or let that person down. The topic is, "A Time Someone Trusted Me."

Summary Discussion Questions:
1. What would life be like if you couldn't trust anyone?
2. What advantages do you have when people trust you?
3. When you lose someone's trust, can you get it back? How?

Topic Variations:
A Time I Didn't Trust Someone

Someone I Can Trust

I Stood Up for Something I Strongly Believe In
A Sharing Circle

Purpose
To describe incidents that demonstrate personal integrity; to explain the connection between integrity and trustworthiness.

Introduce the Topic:
Today's topic is, "I Stood Up for Something I Strongly Believe In." Most of us have experienced at least once the necessity to take a stand concerning something. Standing up for a belief can be difficult, especially if friends or family do not agree with us. Even when they do agree, it is not necessarily easy to state our beliefs publicly. Think of a time when this happened to you.

Maybe you saw others doing something that you felt was wrong, and you confronted them. Perhaps you were involved in a discussion about a controversial subject, and you stated your views, even though they were unpopular. You may remember being nervous and worrying about what might happen or what someone would think. Or you may have felt very sure of yourself. Perhaps when you look back on the occasion, you recall a sense of pride, accomplishment, or even daring. If the outcome was different from what you wanted, tell us what you learned from the experience. Remember, don't mention any names. The topic is, "I Stood Up for Something I Strongly Believe In."

Summary Discussion Questions:
1. What similarities were there in our reasons for standing up for what we believe in?
2. How is standing up for your beliefs similar to being loyal to your friends?
3. What does standing up for your beliefs have to do with being trustworthy?
4. How do you feel about people who refuse to stand up for their beliefs?

Topic Variations:
A Time I Was Afraid to Express My Opinion

I Spoke Out Against Something I Thought Was Wrong

It Was Hard to Say No, But I Did

Someone I Know Who Has Courage
A Sharing Circle

Purpose:
To describe courageous deeds; to recognize courage as a moral value.

Introduce the Topic:
Our topic today is, "Someone I Know Who Has Courage." Courage is mental or moral strength, the will to hold one's own in the face of hardship or danger; it is exceptionally strong determination. Most people show courage at one time or another. Some people are courageous a great deal of the time. Try to think of someone you know — or know about — who shows courage. Perhaps you know a person who risked his or her life to help someone who was in danger. Or you might have in mind a person whose job is risky, like a police officer or a fire fighter. There are many ways to show courage. People who keep working toward their goals despite illness, disability, or other hardships show courage. Often it takes courage to refuse to follow the crowd, and to stand up for what you believe is right. Striving for excellence in almost any area takes courage. Think about Olympic athletes and scientists who work for years trying to find cures for diseases. Take a few moments to think about it. The topic is, "Someone I Know Who Has Courage."

Summary Discussion Questions:
1. How do people learn to be courageous?
2. Why do we admire people who show courage?
3. What have you learned from this discussion about how you can show courage?

Topic Variations:
I Got Up My Courage and Did It

I Wanted to Do Something, But Didn't Have the Courage

I Kept At It Until It Was Done

I Set a Goal and Achieved It

Respect

Respect means showing regard for the worth of someone or something. It includes respect for self (self-esteem), respect for others, and respect for the environment, including other life forms. All other varieties of respect are outgrowths of these three. Respecting someone's property, for example, extends from respecting the owner of the property.

Respect is a *restraining* value. It tells us what *not* to do. When we urge children to respect each other's privacy, we mean don't interfere or interrupt. When we admonish students to respect school property, we mean don't misuse equipment, don't deface walls, don't damage buildings.

When we teach students to show respect, we prevent them from hurting what they ought to value. If we are completely successful, they will end up valuing that for which they have demonstrated respect.

Other ways to foster respect include:

- Create a democratic classroom environment, in which the rights of all students are respected. Show your own regard for every student, every day.

- Expect students to be polite and courteous. Consistently model the use of "please," "thank you," "excuse me," etc.

- Really listen to the opinions and contributions of students. Make it a rule that students listen respectfully to each other.

- Show your appreciation for diversity. Create an environment in which individual differences are celebrated, and where all students feel included and interdependent.

- Teach students a simple decision-making process and encourage them to use it. Respect their ability to make decisions for themselves. Serve as their advisor and consultant.

- When students have difficulty understanding how their behavior affects others, suggest that they apply the classic test of *reversibility*. Ask them: *Would you want to receive this kind of treatment?*

R-E-S-P-E-C-T: What It Means to Me!
Identifying Feelings Through Stories

Purpose:
To help students define the moral value of respect, and distinguish respect from fear.

Materials:
The words *Respect*, and *Fear* written on two signs (one word per sign); masking tape; writing materials for the students; a cassette player and cassette recording of Aretha Franklin's "R-E-S-P-E-C-T" (optional)

Procedure:
Without preliminaries, intrigue the students by asking them to listen, and maybe even dance, to a song. Play Aretha Franklin's famous version of "R-E-S-P-E-C-T" (if available).

After enjoying the recording, engage the students in a brief discussion about the song and its meaning. (Flanklin wants her man to treat her right and literally spells out what that means to her.)

Show the students the sign with "Respect" written on it. Without defining the term, ask them, "Do you appreciate being treated with respect?" Listen to their responses before commenting:

The word "respect" may mean different things to different people. People sometimes experience other feelings and mistake them for respect. Here's one of those other feelings:

Show the students the sign with "Fear" written on it and ask them: *Have you ever heard people say they respected someone, or a group, when they really feared the person or group? If so, tell us about it, but please don't mention any names.*

Listen to the responses of the students, clarifying the distinctions between respect and fear. Then, explain the activity:

We're going to get good at distinguishing between respect and fear. This means we will become clear about which one is which. I'm going to place the "Respect" sign on one wall in the classroom, and the "Fear" sign on another wall. Then I'm going to read a short description of a person or situation. After I finish reading, get up and go stand under the sign that describes how the first person in the story really feels about the person or group I read about. Don't worry if other students select a different sign than you do. You have a right to your opinion and we respect it. If you change your mind and move to another sign we will respect that, too.

Post the signs on two of the classroom walls. One by one, read the situations on the next page. After each reading, give the students time to stand under the sign that best describes the feelings of the first character in the story. As soon as all of the students have decided where to stand, ask each group why they selected that sign, and listen to their responses.

Situations

Kim and Bill have lived next door to each other for years and they know each other's family well. Kim lives with her parents and younger brother in a nice house. Recently her father was laid off from his job and the whole family has been trying to help. Kim's mother has taken on an extra job and Kim is doing her best to take her mother's place at home whenever she can. She keeps things neat and clean and often prepares food. Bill is disappointed one day when he asks Kim to go bike-riding with him and she says she is too busy at home. But the main feeling Bill has for Kim is __?__. (RESPECT)

~

Sarah is reading the story of Huck Finn by Mark Twain, the part about how bad Huck's Dad treated him. At the start of the book, Huck's Dad comes back to town suddenly and, when he finds Huck, beats him up and drags him away from the foster home where he's been living with two nice old ladies. Huck's father is very drunk and later tries to kill Huck, but doesn't even remember it the next day when he wakes up. Sarah knows how she would feel about her father if he were like Huck's. She would feel __?__. (FEAR)

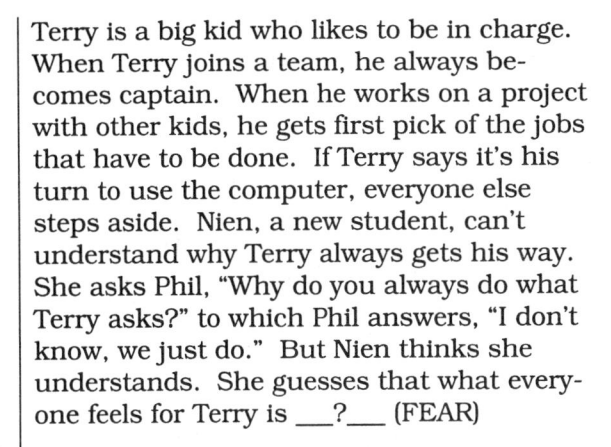

~

Terry is a big kid who likes to be in charge. When Terry joins a team, he always becomes captain. When he works on a project with other kids, he gets first pick of the jobs that have to be done. If Terry says it's his turn to use the computer, everyone else steps aside. Nien, a new student, can't understand why Terry always gets his way. She asks Phil, "Why do you always do what Terry asks?" to which Phil answers, "I don't know, we just do." But Nien thinks she understands. She guesses that what everyone feels for Terry is __?__ (FEAR)

~

Sergio watches the other boys in his neighborhood pick on a new kid named Sam, who is the shortest sixth grader he's ever seen. While this is happening, Sergio notices Sam looking at the boys in a serious way. He doesn't yell or cry and he doesn't even show fear, although Sergio knows that in Sam's place *he* would be afraid. Finally Sam says, "Okay, okay, you guys. I'm new. I'm short. But I'm not a bad guy to have around. After you get to know me, you'll like me." This surprises the boys so much they start to laugh. They tease Sam some more and then they leave him alone. How do you suppose this causes Sergio to feel about Sam? (RESPECT)

Direct the students to form teams of about four members each. Distribute writing materials and explain:

Now it's your turn. Talk with the members of your team and work together to come up with a situation in which someone either respects or fears another person or group. Then select a recorder to write a description of the situation. Later, we will listen to each team's situation and decide which emotion the person in the story is feeling.

After the teams have developed their situations, have each team's recorder read the situation to the class. Then, have the class stand and go to the sign that best describes how the person in the story feels. Allow a spokesperson for the team that developed the situation to ask the students on what basis they made their selections. Lead the class in a culminating discussion.

Discussion Questions:
1. What does it mean to have respect for another person? ...for oneself? ...for the environment?
2. If you respect a person, do you also respect that person's property? Explain your reasoning.
3. What are some examples of "common courtesy" (saying please, thank you, excuse me; waiting one's turn, etc.) and how do they relate to respect?
4. How do we learn to respect others?
5. Why is respect for others necessary in a civilized society?

Adaptations:
With primary-age children, omit the team assignment, ending the activity after the students have responded to the four situations provided. Talk with the students about the differences between respect and fear. Then have them draw pictures of situations in which someone is having respectful or fearful feelings toward others.

A Recipe for Respect
Identifying Respectful Behaviors

Purpose:
This activity helps students gain a clearer understanding of respect by discriminating between behaviors that are respectful and disrespectful, and by generating examples of their own.

Materials:
five descriptions of respectful behavior and five descriptions of disrespectful behavior written on ten tagboard strips about 30 inches long (see below); one blank tagboard strip about 30 inches long per student and one magic marker for every four students; one large mixing bowl labeled "Respectful Actions" and a wooden spoon; one wastepaper basket labeled "Disrespectful Actions"

Procedure:
In preparation for this activity, write brief descriptions of respectful and disrespectful behaviors on the tagboard strips. As much as possible, use examples of behaviors that you have observed among the students in your class. Randomly mix the tagboard strips together and place them upside down in a stack. Here are some examples:

Respectful behavior:
- Greeting people when they walk in the room.
- Looking at people when they talk to you.
- Listening to someone who is speaking to you.
- Offering to share your lunch or snack with someone.
- Saying I'm sorry after bumping into someone.

Disrespectful behavior:
- Not saying hello to someone who has greeted you.
- Laughing at someone who has stumbled.
- Borrowing something from someone without permission.
- Walking away from someone who is talking to you.
- Not saying I'm sorry after bumping into someone.

Introduce the activity by showing the class the mixing bowl (twirl the wooden spoon around in it) and the wastepaper basket. Point out the labels attached to these items, and have the students read them with you. In your own words, explain:

We have been talking about respect — what it is and what it isn't. Today, we're going to create a "Recipe for Respect." Probably the best way to understand respect is to know which actions are respectful and which are disrespectful. I have some descriptions of both kinds of actions here (hold up the 10 tagboard strips you prepared) and I'm going to need your help in deciding whether an action is respectful or disrespectful. If it's respectful, it should go into our bowl, the "Recipe for Respect," and if it's disrespectful, it should go out with the trash.

Hold up one of the tagboard strips and read it together. Ask the class where it should be placed and why.

Distribute the nine remaining tagboard strips to nine students. One by one, allow the students to read their strips to the class, drop them into the bowl or trash basket, and explain their judgments.

Divide the students into teams of four, and provide each student with a blank tagboard strip. Distribute the magic markers. Explain the assignment:

Now it's your turn to come up with actions that are respectful and disrespectful, and write them down on tagboard strips. Your team should generate examples of two respectful actions and two disrespectful ones. When all of the teams have written down their actions, every student will come to the front of the class, show and read one example, place it in the bowl or the trash basket, and explain why you put it there.

As the students generate their statements, circulate and assist with composition, spelling, etc. Then facilitate the sharing and selection process outlined above, making sure each student explains his/her reasoning.

Ceremoniously take the "Disrespectful Actions" out to the school dumpster and let the students dump them in. Prepare a bulletin board in the classroom or cafeteria with the banner, "A Recipe for Respect." Allow the students to post the "Respectful Actions" under the banner. Have them draw and post pictures of cooking utensils and food items to add a clever note.

Discussion Questions:
1. Why do we want to "throw away" disrespectful actions?
2. What would our world be like if all people were respectful of one another?
3. Do you think people should be required to earn respect, or do you think all people are entitled to respect? Explain your reasoning.

Adaptations:
Arrange for two or three upper-grade students who have experienced this activity in their own class to conduct it with children in primary classrooms. Help the older students prepare by supplying them with needed materials and reviewing with them the steps of the activity.

The Best Kind of Friendship Includes Respect
Drawing and Writing

Purpose:
As the name of this activity implies, respect is a critically important ingredient in friendship. This becomes clear to students as they contemplate healthy friendships through art and writing.

Materials:
art materials of your choosing; writing materials

Procedure:
Prior to beginning the activity, write the following words on the chalkboard:
trustworthy
loyal
responsible
honest
kind
considerate
sensitive
generous
fair
caring
dignified

Introduce the activity by telling the students about a childhood friendship you had with an individual you greatly respected. Describe the individual using adjectives similar to those listed on the board. Include an anecdote or two to illustrate the character of your friend and emphasize the degree to which this person's actions and attributes caused you to respect him/her. Answer any questions the students have while continuing to illustrate the importance of respect between friends.

In your own words, ask the students:

Does this make you think of someone you really like and respect? Close your eyes and bring someone to mind. (Pause for a few moments.) Perhaps you can think of a time when this person made you proud that he or she was your friend. Maybe you found out how your friend helped someone who needed help, kept a promise, met a responsibility, told the truth when it needed to be told, or stuck up for you. Perhaps you remember a nerve-wracking situation that your friend handled very well, when others might have gone to pieces.

Listen to the students' responses. Then explain that they are going to draw pictures illustrating these friendships. In your own words, explain:

Show something your friend did — an action that caused you to respect him or her. You can put yourself in the picture, too. Perhaps you want to illustrate something very meaningful that your friend did for you. This friend does not have to be your age; he or she can be a family member, someone older or younger than you, even an adult — anyone whom you respect and consider a friend.

Circulate as the students draw, engaging them in conversation about their illustrations. Suggest they consider using cartoon-style speech bubbles to show what is being said.

Distribute writing materials and instruct the students to tell the same story in words. Point to the adjectives on the chalkboard and read them together, urging the students to use any that describe their friend. Tell them to explain who their friend is, how the friendship started, how long it has lasted, and why they respect this person. Give some examples:

I respect Cindy a lot because she is usually kind and considerate to other people. She is always one of the first to be friendly to new kids at school.

I respect Hahn because he is honest and fair, and can be trusted to keep his promises. He promised to help me with fractions and now I'm doing much better in math.

As the students write, circulate and offer assistance and encouragement. Conclude the activity by inviting individual students to read their stories and show their illustrations to the class. Allow the class to ask questions and offer positive comments at the end of each presentation. Make your own positive comment to each child as well. Finally, collect the illustrations and stories and prepare a display including each student's illustration placed above his/her written story, under the banner: "Friends We Respect and Why"

Discussion Questions:
1. What are some reasons we gave for respecting our friends?
2. Do the friends we described show respect for others? What are some of their respectful behaviors?
3. Why is it important to show respect for others?

Adaptations:
For primary-level children, prepare and duplicate a template consisting of the following sentences. Have the children complete the sentences with your assistance or that of other students. Substitute this handout for the writing assignment described above, and complete the remainder of the activity as written.

I like and respect my friend,

_____

He/She is a _____ person.

One time he/she _____

_____

_____

Respectful Responses
Comparative Role Plays and Discussion

Purpose:
By participating in a series of role plays, the students identify and practice responding to others respectfully in social situations.

Materials:
a container (basket or box) containing role directions written on slips of paper (see pages 46-47)

Procedure:
Prepare for this activity by writing the role directions on slips of paper and placing them in the container.

Announce that the students are going to role play the use of respectful behaviors — actions that demonstrate courtesy and high regard for others.

Invite twelve students to draw role descriptions from the container; tell them to read the descriptions silently and not to share them with anyone. As you do this, explain to the class that you are casting the roles for three different scenarios. Point out that each role description is numbered 1, 2, or 3, and that these designations indicate in which scenario the actors will participate.

Have the three casts meet for 15 minutes to plan and rehearse. Tell them to prepare two scenarios: one showing disrespectful behaviors in the situation, and the other showing respectful actions.

Direct the students who do not receive acting parts to be careful observers of the dramatizations. Tell them that they will have opportunities to demonstrate additional respectful behaviors following the positive versions of the scenarios.

Meet briefly with each team to clarify its scenario.

Moderate the presentations, giving enough advance information about each scenario to enable the audience to understand what is going on. To maximize comparisons, have each team present its respectful version immediately following its disrespectful version. After the respectful version, ask audience members to come forward and demonstrate additional respectful actions that could be used in situations like the one dramatized. Facilitate discussion following each role play.

Discussion Questions:
At the end of each role play showing disrespectful behavior, ask the class:
1. What happened in this role play that was disrespectful?
2. What caused the disrespectful behavior?
3. How did the disrespectful behaviors cause others in the scenario to feel? How would you have felt in a situation like this?

At the end of each role play showing respectful behavior, ask the class:
1. What respectful actions did you observe in this scenario?
2. Did the respectful behaviors require any special skills? What were they and how can they be learned?
3. How did the respectful actions make others feel? How would you have felt in this situation?

Adaptations:

Arrange for a team of the upper-grade students who have experienced this activity in their own class to conduct it with primary-level children. Help the older students prepare to lead the activity and, especially, the follow-up discussions. Make sure they understand the key concepts they are trying to get across.

Scenario #1: "Introductions." A student is in the grocery store with his/her mother or father. They encounter the child's teacher. The teacher and the parent have never met each other. Since the child knows both of them, the respectful action would be to introduce them to each other in a friendly way.

Role-Play Descriptions for Scenario #1:

> #1 Play yourself. You are with one of your parents at the grocery store.

> #1 Play the teacher of this class, shopping for groceries.

> #1 Play the mother or father of a student. You are with your child at the grocery store.

Scenario #2: "Greetings, Thank You's, and Goodbyes." One student is having a birthday and the student's parents are giving him/her a party. One-by-one, three invited students arrive. The scenario should include what happens as each child arrives and what happens after the party is over and each child leaves. Respectful behavior includes warm greetings, sincere thank you's and friendly good-byes.

Role-Play Descriptions for Scenario #2:

#2 Play yourself arriving at a birthday party.

#2 Play yourself arriving at a birthday party.

#2 Play yourself arriving at a birthday party.

#2 Play yourself. It's your birthday and your parents are hosting a birthday party for you.

#2 Play a mother hosting a birthday party for your son or daughter.

#2 Play a father hosting a birthday party for your son or daughter.

Scenario #3: "Disagreements." Two students are writing a story together and decide to use the word *license*. Both students insist that they are spelling the word correctly. Since a dictionary is not available, they go to another child who is a good speller and ask for help.

Role-Play Descriptions for Scenario #3:

#3 Play yourself. You and a friend are writing a story together, and want to use the word *license*. You incorrectly spell LISENCE, but you believe you have spelled the word right.

#3 Play yourself. You and a friend are writing a story together and want to use the word *license*. Your friend incorrectly spells LISENCE. You know it is wrong and say so.

#3 Play a student who is a good speller. Two of your friends are writing a story and are having a disagreement about how to spell the word *license*. They come to you for help.

Your Rights Deserve Respect
Team Presentations and Discussion

Purpose:
Through research and creative team presentations, the students explain the history and intent of five basic human rights and the U.S. Bill of Rights.

Materials:
a copy of The Bill of Rights of the United States of America; five dictionaries; art and writing materials

Procedure:
Prior to leading this activity, write the words *Liberty, Justice, Autonomy, Privacy*, and *Dignity* on the chalkboard.

Introduce the activity by asking the students what it means when someone has a "right" to something. Listen to their responses, paraphrase as necessary to clarify meaning, and express your appreciation to each child who responds. Then look up the word "right" in the dictionary and read the applicable definition to the class. In your own words, explain:

We have been learning a lot recently about respect. Rights and respect go hand-in-hand. When you respect someone, you do not knowingly violate, or hurt that person's rights in any way. You protect his or her rights, and you object if anyone tries to take them away. People who truly respect you do the same for you. Furthermore, if you respect yourself, you stand up to anyone who tries to violate or take away your rights, unless doing so endangers you. But let's be sure we know what we're talking about. What exactly are our "rights?"

Point to the five words written on the chalkboard and read them with the students. Explain:

These are five basic human rights. The first two are mentioned in the Pledge of Allegiance. People in many other countries have these rights too, but as Americans each of us is <u>guaranteed</u> these rights, which means that the government promises not to violate them or take them away from us. In addition, our laws help prevent anyone else from violating them or taking them away.

Have the students form six teams. Assign one of the human rights listed on the board to the first five teams. To the sixth team, assign the U.S. Bill of Rights. Explain that each team is going to create a way to explain the meaning of its assigned right to the rest of the class. The sixth team is to study the Bill of Rights and explain to the class how it came to be written and what it means. Suggest that students use art, music, drama, or any other method to get their message across. One possibility is to show what happens when the right is violated and when it is respected.

Help the teams get started. Distribute dictionaries to five of the teams and the copy of The Bill of Rights to the sixth. Give the teams time to complete research, and to plan, create, and practice their presentations. Circulate as the teams work, consulting with them and assisting as needed.

As the teams make their presentations to the class, help them only if absolutely necessary. (In some cases you may need to serve as a narrator or the initiator of discussion.) Encourage the class to ask each presenting team questions following its presentation. After all of the teams have made their reports to the class, bring closure to the activity by asking the questions below.

Discussion Questions:

1. When you respect someone's rights, what are some ways you almost always show it?
2. When you respect someone's rights, what are some things you *never* do to that person?
3. Should the rights of every person automatically be given full respect or should individuals earn that respect? Explain.

Adaptations:

With primary-age children, examine "The Pledge of Allegiance" with the goal of figuring out together what it really means. When you come to the words, "liberty" and "justice," define them for the children at their level of understanding. Provide examples of situations where people enjoy liberty and justice and other examples where they do not. Ask the children to illustrate the pledge. Help each child write a sentence at the bottom of his/her picture that explains the meaning of the illustration.

Our Most Respected Heroes
Interviews and Reports

Purpose:
Through interviews and research, the students identify heroic individuals, and describe their actions and the qualities and characteristics that lead to heroic deeds.

Materials:
Access to a library with encyclopedias and biographies of heroic figures; current issues of magazines such as *Time* and *Life*; writing materials

Procedure:
Introduce this activity by showing the class two or three written descriptions of the lives and deeds of heroic individuals, some more well-known than others. These might include: (1) a biography located in the school library of a famous hero or heroine, (2) an encyclopedia with a page marked offering a description of a noted person's life, and (3) a popular magazine, such as *Time*, or *Life*, with a story about an exceptional, but perhaps rather "ordinary" person. In your own words, explain:

Almost everyone is interested in people, alive or dead, who have done something unusual. If the unusual thing they have done inspires our admiration and respect, we often call them heroes or heroines. They interest and inspire us; we talk about them and write about them so their stories won't be forgotten. Let me show you some examples.

After showing the class each book and/or article, explain that you want each student to "play detective" by conducting an investigation. Their task is to interview a parent, grandparent, other relative, teacher, neighbor, or friend. They should start by explaining that the interview is for a school assignment, and then ask: "Who is one of your most respected heroes or heroines — someone alive or dead whom you admire and respect?" Instruct the students to listen and take notes, being careful to find out what the hero did (or does) that is so impressive.

Once the students have a verbal account of the hero, direct them to find written information in magazines or books at home or in the library. Tell them to find out what makes this person so remarkable and deserving of admiration and respect.

Have the students prepare a written report of their findings. From the written report, ask them to develop a brief oral report. Both reports should include:
- a description of the impressive actions of the hero or heroine
- the identity of the interviewee who first mentioned this person
- the *student's* feelings about the hero/heroine after completing the research and writing

After all of the students have given their oral reports, ask several questions to facilitate a summary discussion, writing the responses of the students on the chalkboard.

Discussion Questions:
1. Most (or all) of the people we've reported on are famous in some way. Can an ordinary person be a hero? Explain.
2. What kinds of actions were our interviewees most impressed with?
3. What qualities and characteristics caused our heroes to do the things they did?
4. How do people get these qualities and characteristics — are they just born with them or do they learn them as they grow up?

Adaptations:
In addition to writing two or three sentences about the hero or heroine of their choice, ask primary children to draw a picture of the hero doing the thing for which s/he is renowned. The oral reports should focus on what these illustrations depict.

A Friend I Respect
A Sharing Circle

Purpose:
To identify attributes and specific behaviors that earn the respect of others.

Introduce the Topic:
Our topic today is, "A Friend I Respect." Do you have a friend you like? (Listen to the children's responses.) Do you have a friend you not only like, but respect as well? (Again, listen to responses.) Maybe you both like and respect the same person. In fact, that's the best kind of friendship — one in which each person likes and respects the other. But perhaps we should stop for a moment and talk about what respect is. People respect other people when they know they can trust them, when they are loyal, and when they do what they say they will do. Most of us respect people who are kind and considerate of others, who tell the truth even when its tough to do, and who handle problems without acting crazy. Tell us about a friend of yours who fits one or more of these descriptions. Think about it for a few moments. The topic is, "A Friend I Respect."

Summary Discussion Questions:
1. How important is it that people respect as well as like their friends?
2. Is it important to you that your friends respect you? Why?
3. What did you learn from this discussion about how to be respected?

Topic Variations:
A Friend I Can Trust Who Trusts Me

I Have a Friend I Respect Who Is a Family Member

An Adult Friend I Respect

I Have a Friend Who Respects Me Because...

A Hero I Respect
A Sharing Circle

Purpose:
To encourage the students to identify people they greatly admire, and to describe admirable qualities in those people.

Introduce the Topic:
Our topic for this circle is, "A Hero I Respect." Actually, since women heroes are sometimes called "heroines," the topic is really, "A Hero or Heroine I Respect." As you look back at the people you've read and heard about who have done admirable and courageous things, which one stands out in your mind? Maybe you are impressed by a hero or heroine who stood up for people's rights, or one who had the courage to say or do things that no one else would do. Perhaps your hero risked her life to save a child, or devoted his life to discovering a cure for some disease. Your chosen hero may be one of the people we've studied in class, or it could be someone you know — a relative or friend whom you greatly admire. Give it some thought. Tell us who your hero or heroine is and what that person did to earn your admiration. Our topic is, "A Hero or Heroine I Respect."

Summary Discussion Questions:
1. How are our heroes alike? How are they different?
2. Why do people have heroes and heroines?
3. What do heroes teach us?

Topic Variations:
A Time I Took a Stand for Something I Believed In

When Someone in My Family Did Something Heroic

A Time I Was a Hero or Heroine to Someone

I Respected Myself for Something I Did
A Sharing Circle

Purpose:
To identify specific behaviors that earn the respect of self and others.

Introduce the Topic:
We have been learning about respect — what it is and why people appreciate being treated respectfully. We've learned that certain actions are respectful and that some people are particularly deserving of respect because they have done things we admire.

Our topic for this circle is, "I Respected Myself for Something I Did." This is a very important topic because it reminds us that the person who most needs our respect is ourself. Sometimes we do things that make us feel particularly proud. Think of a time when you did something you were very pleased with. Maybe you helped someone who needed and wanted your help, or perhaps you were tempted to do something that might have hurt someone, like gossiping or telling a secret, but you stopped yourself. Maybe you told the truth, even though it was hard, or refused to go along when other kids did something wrong. Think about it for a few moments. The topic is, "I Respected Myself for Something I Did."

Summary Discussion Questions:
1. What kinds of actions cause self-respect?
2. Why is it important to respect yourself?
3. If you don't respect yourself, is it likely that other people will respect you? Why or why not?

Topic Variations:
I Felt Proud of Myself When...

How My Respect for Someone Increased His/Her Self-Respect

A Way I Show Respect for Others
A Sharing Circle

Purpose:
To describe specific behaviors that demonstrate respect for others.

Introduce the Topic:
We talk a lot about treating people with respect. But what exactly does that mean? In our circle today, we're going to discuss specific respectful actions. The topic is, "A Way I Show Respect for Others."

You probably show respect in many ways. Try to think of the one you use most often and describe it to us. Maybe you show respect by being courteous or polite. Perhaps you make it a point to listen carefully to others without interrupting. Or maybe you never intentionally hurt or take advantage of anyone. Do you avoid telling other people what to do because you respect their right to make their own decisions? Do you show tolerance for people who are different from you, and encourage your friends to do the same? Think about this topic for a few moments. When you are ready to share, tell us about, "A Way I Show Respect for Others."

Summary Discussion Questions:
1. What similarities did you hear in the ways we show respect?
2. How can you tell when someone respects you?
3. How can we help each other improve skills like politeness and courtesy?

Topic Variations:
A Time I Wanted Respect, But Didn't Get It

A Time I Earned the Respect of Someone Important

How I Show Respect for My Friends

A Way I Show Respect for My Parent

People Seem to Respect Me When...
A Sharing Circle

Purpose:
To identify qualities and behaviors that inspire respectful attitudes in others.

Introduce the Topic:
Our topic today is one of those unfinished sentences. Your job is to complete the sentence with something that is true for you. The topic is, "People Seem to Respect Me When..."

Have you ever noticed that certain things seem to inspire more admiration and respect than others? When do people treat you with the greatest respect? Is it when you speak out about an opinion or belief? Or do people seem to respect you most when you accomplish something, like finish a project, get a good grade, or score points in a game. Maybe you've noticed that you receive respect when you have the courage to tell the truth. Or perhaps respect comes to you when you help others. Think about it for a few moments. Tell us the circumstances under which you receive respect, and how being respected causes you to feel. The topic is, "People Seem to Respect Me When..."

Summary Discussion Questions:
1. How does the respect you show for others affect the amount of respect you receive?
2. Do all people deserve respect, regardless of what they do or don't do? Explain.
3. What do we mean when we say "respect property" or "respect each other's space"?

Topic Variations:
I Respect Others When...

A Time I Was Disrespectful

A Time Someone Was Disrespectful Toward Me

Responsibility

Responsibility means literally, *ability to respond.* It is an *active* value, compelling us to help others, fulfill our obligations, and contribute to the community and society.

Responsibility is also closely related to trustworthiness, in that it implies being dependable, keeping commitments and not letting others down.

Acting responsibly requires taking into consideration the consequences of various alternatives before choosing a course of action. How will everyone involved be affected? Once a decision is made, it means taking responsibility for the outcome, even if the outcome bears little resemblance to what was predicted.

To encourage responsibility in your students:

- Model responsibility by fulfilling your own obligations to the very best of your ability. Present well-planned lessons. Teach with energy and enthusiasm. Give extra help to students who are having trouble.

- Teach a decision-making process that encourages students to make conscious choices from among alternatives that have been examined not only for their relative effectiveness in achieving a goal, but for their consequences.

- Use a similar process to help students solve problems democratically. Require that students consider minority views and attempt to achieve consensus.

- Use cooperative learning to teach children how to work interdependently, doing their part, helping and including others, and sharing responsibility.

- Expect students to be thorough and accurate in completing assignments. Award grades fairly, based on merit.

- Encourage service learning in the classroom by regularly utilizing messengers, monitors, clean-up helpers, and tutors. Encourage students to team up with "homework buddies" and to become participants in cooperative learning projects.

- Give students opportunities to respond to moral issues. Ask them:
—*What is the responsible thing to do in this situation?*
—*Who behaved responsibly? Who didn't?*
—*Who was responsible for what happened in this situation?*
—*Would you want to be treated like this? Why or why not?*
—*Would you want all people to act this way in situations similar to this one? Why or why not?*

What Is Responsibility?
Using Literature to Build a Definition

Purpose:
By listening to and discussing well-known stories, and drawing and writing about responsible story characters, the students define *responsibility* and describe responsible actions.

Materials:
classic, well-known literature selections that clearly illustrate responsibility on the part of one or more characters (*The Little Engine That Could, Horton Hatches the Who, The Wizard of Oz*); dictionary; art and writing materials; tagboard and magic markers; a banner that reads, "Responsible Action Is:"

Procedure:
Begin by telling the students that you have a challenge for them. Then write the word, *Responsibility* on the chalkboard, read it with the students, and talk about its meaning.

Listen to the response of each child who wishes to offer a definition, and then point out that the word itself gives an important clue. Ask the students, "Do you see two smaller words here?" Discuss the words, *response* and *ability*, and help the students recognize that responsibility means, literally, the ability to respond or take action.

Using the input of the students, write an initial definition on the chalkboard. Then, look up *responsibility* in the dictionary and see if the definition matches that which the students derived through discussion. Note key differences.

Use literature to provide examples of responsible actions. Read a story to the students, or read passages from a story with which they are already familiar. Then ask:
— *Who acted in a responsible way in this story?*
— *Was anyone not responsible (or irresponsible)?*
— *In what ways did (name of character) act responsibly?*
— *How would you feel if you were... (one of the children who would not get toys if the Little Engine was not so responsible?; the baby in the egg who would not hatch if Horton didn't keep it warm?; Dorothy and you didn't have the Scarecrow, Tin Woodsman, or Cowardly Lion to help you get to the Emerald City?)*
— *How do you feel about the characters who were irresponsible?*

Ask the students to think of a story they like in which a character demonstrates responsible action, and to draw a picture illustrating that character being responsible. Below their drawing, direct the students to write a sentence or paragraph describing the responsible action and how they feel about it. Circulate as the students draw and write, offering encouragement, acknowledgment, and assistance as needed.

Re-direct the students to their initial definition of responsibility and ask them if they believe the definition can be improved. Facilitate further discussion about the meaning of responsibility, adding words to the definition, or writing a clarifying sentence or two on the board.

Write the revised definition on tagboard and post it at the top of a bulletin board under a banner reading, "Responsible Action Is:" Complete the display by posting the children's illustrations.

Discussion Questions:
1. Does responsible action just happen or do we do it on purpose? Explain.
2. Is an action responsible if it is sloppy or poorly done? Why or why not?
3. What do we need to do to be thought of as responsible people?

Taking Responsibility
Brainstorming and Committing to Responsible Behaviors

Purpose:
To encourage the students to publicly accept responsibility for positive actions at school and home, to self-report their progress, and to receive acknowledgment for keeping their commitments.

Materials:
descriptions of 10 responsible classroom behaviors written on tagboard strips about 30 inches long; one blank 30-inch tagboard strip per student and one magic marker for every one to four students; three boxes, one labeled, "We all take responsibility," the second labeled, "Some of us take responsibility," and the third labeled, "One person takes responsibility;" self-stick labels; a banner reading, "We Take Responsibility"

Procedure:
Prepare the tagboard strips in advance. Mix the strips together and place them face down on a surface at the front of the classroom. Use the following examples, or list responsible behaviors that are more relevant to your classroom.

Responsible Behaviors:
- Walking into the classroom quietly.
- Trying not to bother others.
- Putting things back where they belong.
- Putting trash in the wastebasket.
- Listening to the teacher or student who is speaking.
- Bringing in play equipment after recess and lunch.
- Cleaning and straightening the bookshelves.
- Erasing the chalkboard at the end of the school day.
- Taking all books back to the library twice a week.
- Distributing and collecting special materials.

Introduce the activity by showing the class the stack of cardboard strips and the three boxes. Read the labels together. Explain in your own words:

We have been learning about a very important kind of action — responsible action. Now we are going to go a step further. Each of you is going to promise in front of the class to do at least one responsible action. I have written some tasks and behaviors on tagboard strips and you are going to have a chance to write some, too. But first let's decide in which box to place each of these actions, and let people volunteer to take responsibility for them.

One by one, show the strips to the children, reading each one aloud with them. Ask the students to decide if the behavior described is something all students should do, some should do, or only one child needs to do. As each behavior requiring total class commitment is read, ask the students to join together and say the words, "I take responsibility to..." and then read in unison the behavior written on the strip. Ask volunteers to accept responsibility for those behaviors that the class agrees require only one or a few students. Ask the volunteers to pledge, "I take responsibility for... ." Jot the name of each volunteer on the back of the appropriate tagboard strip. Place all strips in the correct box.

Distribute the blank tagboard strips and magic markers. Tell the students that you want each of them to think of a responsible behavior to commit to carrying out at school or at home. Brainstorm examples and list them on the board. Ask the students to think about:
- responsible behaviors that make the classroom enjoyable for everyone.
- tasks and responsibilities that need to be done at school
- tasks and responsibilities that need to be done at home and are helpful to parents.
- caring for pets responsibly.
- taking care of equipment and possessions.

As the students take turns using the magic markers, allow them to help each other with wording and spelling. Circulate to lend your own assistance as well.

Have the students categorize these responsible actions into the same three categories as they did the first group. Ask each child to publicly pledge to take responsibility for the behavior described on his/her tagboard strip.

Prepare a display of the responsible actions under the banner, "We Take Responsibility!" Place the strips listing behaviors that everyone committed to in a column down the center of the display area. Make two more columns — one containing the behaviors that require the commitment of several students, and the other listing the behaviors for which one student has volunteered. Around the behaviors in these last two categories, cluster the names of committed students written on self-stick labels.

Facilitate periodic follow-up discussions, focusing on the progress of students in keeping their commitments. Acknowledge and reinforce responsible behavior.

Discussion Questions:
1. How do you feel when you do the thing you pledged to do?
2. What problems have you had keeping your commitment?
3. Do you think it helped to make your commitment in front of the class? Explain.

Adaptations:
With primary-age children, carry out this activity as presented; however, on *your* tagboard strips, in addition to the written statements, include pictures of responsible behaviors. If appropriate, ask the children to draw pictures on theirs, too.

Who's Responsible For What?
Stories, Decision Making, and Discussion

Purpose:
To give students practice in 1) making decisions about who bears responsibility in specific situations, and 2) describing alternative responsible behaviors.

Materials:
(optional) one copy of *The Book of Virtues: A Treasury of Great Moral Stories*, edited, with commentary, by William Bennett, New York: Simon and Schuster, 1993

Procedure:
Begin this activity by announcing to the students that you have one or two stories to read (or tell) them. Two excellent stories are summarized below. The original versions of both stories are printed in *The Book of Virtues*.

The Bell of Atri

The king installed a bell in a tower in the Italian town of Atri, and announced to the people that the bell should only be rung when someone felt he or she had been wronged. Through the years, every time the bell was rung, the judges came together to right each wrong. After years of wear and tear, the bell's rope became old, torn, and shortened. This worried the judges, because if a child were wronged, the child would not be able to reach the rope. To solve this problem, a man tied a grapevine to the end of the rope, making it long and strong enough for even the smallest child to operate.

In the hills above Atri lived a man who had been a famous knight when he was younger. He had a great horse who was his best friend and had saved him from many dangers in his knighthood days. But as the man grew older, he became a miser and loved nothing but gold. He sold everything he could for money except his horse, which had grown very old and feeble. The man thought no one wanted the horse, so he turned it out without trying to sell it. The poor horse could barely find enough grass to eat and was slowly starving and freezing from the cold. People ran the horse off and treated it badly.

One day, shortly after the grapevine was tied to the rope of the bell of Atri, the horse was looking for food and wandered near the tower. The horse saw the green leaves on the grapevine and took a bite, which pulled the rope. The bell sounded and it seemed to say, "Someone has done me wrong!" The judges came running and immediately saw the situation: The poor horse was telling the world how it felt in the best way it could. They ordered the old miserly knight brought before them, and made him spend half of his gold on food, a new stable, and a green pasture for his poor old horse.

Icarus and Daedalus

Daedalus was a very famous and clever builder and artist in ancient Greece. King Minos of the nearby island of Crete had a big problem: A minotaur (a horrible monster that was half bull, half man) was on the loose. Minos succeeded in getting Daedalus to come to Crete to build a prison that would hold the beast. Icarus, the young son of Daedalus, went with his father. Daedalus designed and built the prison, but when he and his son wanted to sail back to Greece, Minos imprisoned them in the top of a tower. He wanted Daedalus to be on call to take care of any other problems that might arise.

Being very clever and never giving up, Daedalus came up with a method of escape, which he learned from the sea gulls as he watched them fly. After collecting lots of feathers, he created a huge pair of wings fastened together with string and wax. Then he taught himself to use them. Next, Daedalus made a pair for Icarus, and gave his son flying lessons. Then Daidalus and Icarus waited for the perfect day when the winds would be just right for flying back home to Greece.

When the right day came, father and son prepared to leave, but first Daedalus gave Icarus a warning: "Don't fly too low, because the sea spray will get your wings wet and bog them down, or too high, because the sun's rays will melt the wax. Either way you'll crash. Just stay by me and you'll be fine." As they took off, both were scared, but soon they got used to flying and Icarus in particular became full of joy. He forgot his father's warning and sailed higher and higher.

Daedalus yelled for his son to come back, but Icarus was completely overcome with the urge to get as close to the heavens as he could. Little by little the feathers came off, then all of a sudden the wax melted completely and no matter how much he beat his arms up and down Icarus could not stay aloft; he fell into the sea and drowned. Daedalus, the sad father, finally found his son's body and carried it to Greece for burial. Later he built a temple over the grave in memory of the son he loved so much, who failed to follow his guidance at a crucial time.

After reading (or telling) the stories, engage the students in a discussion concerning who was, or should have been, responsible for what. Help the students recognize three moral lessons illustrated in the stories:
- People are obligated to care for each other and their animals.
- Parents are responsible for guiding their children.
- Children have the responsibility to listen to, and follow, their parent's guidance.

Next, read the scenarios (opposite page) to the students, asking the accompanying questions and facilitating discussion.

Conclude the activity with more questions and a summary discussion.

Discussion Questions:
1. Imagine that you are the little kid having rocks thrown at him in the first scenario, or the person who lost the wallet in the second scenario, or the dog in the third scenario. How would you feel if no one was responsible enough to care about you or help you?
2. Is it always a good idea to help someone who is asking for help? Is helping always the most responsible thing to do?
3. How can you tell if a situation is your responsibility?
4. Why is it important to know who is responsible for what?

Variations:
Have volunteers role play the scenarios, trying out various responsible behaviors. Facilitate discussion.

Tell primary-age children the tale, "The Boy Who Cried Wolf." Then ask them questions tailored to your version. Here are samples:
—*What did the boy do that was not responsible?*
—*Why did all the sheep finally get eaten by the wolves?*
—*If you had been one of the people who lived in the village, would you have believed the boy after he cried "Wolf!" the first two times?*
—*Today, we don't have villages and sheep like the people in the story, but the boy had been given an important job to do. It was his responsibility. Do you think children today can help with important jobs and be responsible?*

From the scenarios, choose examples that younger children can readily relate to. After reading them aloud, ask the children to describe responsible actions in those situations.

Scenarios

① You and your parents are visiting the home of some relatives or friends. One of the boys in the family, who is your age, throws a rock at his little brother. No adults are around at the time.
—*Do you have a responsibility to do anything?*
—*If so, what is the most responsible thing to do?*

② You enter a store with one of your parents, and see a wallet on the floor. You pick up the wallet and look inside. You see that the wallet contains money. Your parent has not noticed any of this.
—*Do you have a responsibility to do anything?*
—*If so, what is the most responsible thing to do?*

③ Your sister begged for a puppy for her birthday and got one. But now it is almost a year later, and she has practically forgotten the dog. She rarely gives him fresh water or feeds or plays with him.
—*What is the most responsible thing to do in this situation?*

④ Your friend comes up to you before school starts and tells you she didn't do her homework and wants to copy yours.
—*Who is responsible for your friend's homework?*
—*What is the best thing for you to do?*

⑤ Your friend is angry at his sister and his Dad. Yesterday, he got into a fight with his sister, which he says was all her fault, but his Dad punished them both. Today, you are at your friend's house and you are thinking about what happened.
—*Do you have any responsibilities in this situation?*

Dear Genie...
Sharing and Solving Problems

Purpose:
To give students an opportunity to share a problem anonymously, and to practice responding with helpful suggestions to the problems of others.

Materials:
A decorated box labeled "Ask the Genie!" with a slit at the top for the insertion of written problems; a not-too-serious, concrete problem of your own written on a piece of paper and folded; writing materials

Procedure:
Intrigue the students by telling them that you have written down a problem which has been bothering you. Show them the folded piece of paper and the box labeled, "Ask the Genie!" Insert the problem through the slit at the top of the box. Then explain the activity in your own words:

One very important way to be responsible is to be willing to help people when they ask for help. I just put a letter in the Genie's box with a description of one of my problems, but I didn't sign the letter. You can do the same if you want to. Sometimes people feel fine about sharing a problem with others, and other times they prefer to be anonymous. In this activity, we will all be anonymous.

Pretend that the box is a magic lamp, with the Genie inside. Tell him about a problem, but remember, this Genie is not magic. He can't make impossible things happen; he can only make suggestions and give advice, which isn't so bad, because it leaves you in control.

Distribute writing materials and allow the students to write down their problems (one per individual) in a letter beginning with the words, "Dear Genie." Direct the students to sign their letters in a way that does not reveal their identity. Have them fold their letters and place them in the box.

The following day, open the box, and have each child take out one letter. Ask the students to form groups of four or five, and to take turns reading aloud the problems they selected. Tell the groups to brainstorm possible solutions to each problem. Suggest that the students not say anything if they hear their own letter being read, but simply participate in the discussion like everyone else.

After the groups brainstorm possible solutions to a problem, direct them to write one or more of the solutions on the back of the letter. Have them sign the response, "Genie." (If you have more problems than "Genies," write responses to excess letters yourself.)

Collect the letters and place them on a table in the back of the room. One at a time or in small groups, allow the students to go to the table and find their letters. Give them time to read the Genie's response to their request for help. Conclude the activity with a summary discussion.

Discussion Questions:
1. How did you feel asking an advice-giving Genie for solutions to your problem?
2. What was it like for you to be the Genie?
3. Is it normal to have problems?
4. When is it okay to ask for help in solving a problem?
5. What good ideas did this activity give you for solving different types of problems?

Adaptations:
Ask primary-age children to make a picture of themselves "having a problem that bothers them." Encourage them to write as much as they can about the problem on the same piece of paper. As the children engage in artistic expression, circulate and converse with each child in a low key manner. Take notes regarding each child's problem. Later, write a short letter to each child on the back of his/her picture. Sign your responses, "The Genie," and return the pictures. Have the children help each other read the Genie's letters.

Everyday Heroes!
Letter-writing and Interviews

Purpose:
Through brainstorming, interviewing, photography and art, the students develop insight concerning the important roles "everyday heroes" (parents, relatives, neighbors, teachers, etc.) play in their own survival and well-being, .

Materials:
art and writing materials; a banner that reads: "Our Everyday Heroes: The Responsible Adults We Know"

Procedure:
Begin this activity by conveying its underlying theme to the students. Use a personal example, or describe a scene from a story or movie that explains this idea: The people who make the most important positive impact on our lives are the responsible ones who nurture us each day of our childhood — our parents, aunts, uncles, teachers, neighbors, and other significant people. Here is an example:

I want to tell you about a scene I once saw in a movie that I'll never forget. The movie is "The Magnificent Seven," and it's about seven American gunmen who go to a little Mexican town to help the poor people fight off a gang of bandits who are stealing everything they have. The little boys in the town think that the gunmen are great, and make them their heroes. In the scene I remember so well, the boys are telling one of the gunmen that he is so much better than their fathers who are only farmers and not as tough as he is. It shocks them when the gunman gets upset and insists that they have it all wrong. He says that he is a coward compared to their fathers, because he never had the strength or the guts to get married, have children, and work hard every day to feed a family.

That scene caused me to realize how true it is that the real heroes and heroines are the people who work every day in regular jobs, do their best to bring up children even though they might not do it perfectly, and hang in there day after day, month after month, year after year. The real heroes and heroines are "everyday heroes" because they are highly responsible. Without them, where would we be?

Listen to the responses of the students. Discuss the fact that "everyday heroes" are so often taken for granted, yet very deserving of acknowledgment and appreciation. Suggest that the students select a person in their own life and plan to interview that person. Explain that you would like the students to help you create a gallery displaying photos and drawings of "everyday heroes."

Together, brainstorm the contents of an introductory letter. Write the letter on the chalkboard. Later, convert it to a template for duplication. Here is a sample letter:

CHARACTER EDUCATION IN AMERICA'S SCHOOLS: Responsibility

Dear _____,

Our class has been talking about the responsible adults we know who work hard every day and do their best to help other people whenever they can. We call these people "everyday heroes."

To me, you are one of these important people. Would you help me by allowing me to interview you? These are the questions I would like you to answer:

1. How did you learn to be a responsible adult?
2. What are the best and the worst things about being an "everyday hero (or heroine)?"
3. Who were your heroes and heroines when you were my age?
4. When you were my age, were any of your heroes "everyday heroes?" If so, who were they?

Thank you,

_____

P.S. Will you give me a recent photo? Or may I draw a picture of you for a gallery display at school?

Have the students sign their letters. Encourage them to take notes during their interviews and to take or obtain photos or draw "portraits" of their interviewees.

Facilitate a class discussion regarding what the students learned as a result of their completed interviews. Chart their responses:

Discussion Questions:
1. How did our interviewees learn to be responsible adults?
2. What did they say is the hardest thing about being a caring, responsible adult?
3. What are their rewards?
4. Who were their heroes (and heroines) when they were your age?
5. Did they have any "everyday heroes?" If so, who were they?

Invite the students to help with the gallery display. Arrange the photos and drawings under the banner, "Our Everyday Heroes: The Responsible Adults We Know." Under each photo/drawing, place a caption with the name of the student interviewer and the "everyday hero."

Adaptations:
To share this concept with primary-age children, move the gallery display of "everyday heroes" to a location where everyone in the school can see it. Give individual students who helped create the display the opportunity to talk to the younger children about it, explaining how it was made and why. Back in the primary classrooms, direct the children to discuss their own "everyday heroes" and to write and deliver thank-you cards to them.

Being Responsible Earns Rights
Story Analysis and Discussion

Purpose:
Through discussion and drama, the students identify and discuss specific rights that are earned and preserved through responsible behavior.

Preparations:
two charts drawn on the chalkboard or whiteboard (see samples on opposite page); chalk or markers

Procedure:
Introduce this activity by asking the students if they remember the story of Chicken Little. Ask them to help you tell it. (The story is about a hen who has a big job. She plants wheat seeds, cultivates and waters them, harvests and grinds them, and finally uses the flour to bake a loaf of bread. During this process she repeatedly asks all of the other animals in the barnyard for help, but they refuse. However, when the bread comes out of the oven they each want some, and Chicken Little refuses to share it with them.)

Ask the students how they feel about Chicken Little's refusal to share the bread she made by herself, without help. Listen respectfully to all of their responses. Then ask:

What she did was not generous, but maybe it was what they deserved. Did her friends really have a right to the bread?

Again, listen to the responses of the students. Then, direct their attention to the board, and to the heading, "Rights We Have Now (That We Didn't Have Before)" In your own words, explain:

You are allowed to do many things now that you were not allowed to do when you were younger. Have you ever wondered why? Perhaps you have the right to decide what you want to wear and put it on yourself, whereas when you were little, you didn't know what to wear and needed help getting dressed.

On the chalkboard, under the heading, "Rights," record the statement: *Decide what to wear and dress myself*

Ask the students what they have done to earn this right. List their responses under the heading, "Reasons." Reasons might include learning to make good decisions, success in dressing, care of clothes, etc.

Ask the students to name additional rights and the reasons they have been granted these rights, and record their statements under these same two headings until about six rights and reasons have been recorded. To the extent possible, focus on rights as a logical outgrowth of responsible behavior.

Ask volunteers to act out impromptu scenarios for the rights listed, recreating the responsible actions that earned each specific right. Allow each volunteer to select the other members of his/her cast. Provide suggestions and coaching, and lead the class in applause after each scenario.

Next, brainstorm a list of rights that the students would like to have in the future and things they can do to show they are responsible enough to be granted those rights. To assist the students in determining how to earn the rights, tell them:

Remember Chicken Little? The other animals didn't deserve to eat the bread because they made no effort to help prepare it. They were not responsible contributors to the work. One of the best ways to prove that you deserve a right is to be a contributor — to show that you are capable. How can you show your willingness to be responsible so that you can earn these rights?

Write the responses of the students on the second chart. Conclude the activity with a summary discussion.

**Rights We Now Have
(That We Didn't Have Before)**
Rights: Reasons:

Discussion Questions:
1. Chicken Little didn't give the other animals bread, but she did give them a lesson. What was it?
2. Why do we have to earn our rights?
3. Do people ever have their rights and privileges taken away? Why?
4. What have you learned from this activity?

Adaptations:
If you are working with primary-age children, read or tell the story of Chicken Little and then talk about its meaning. Ask the children:
— If you were Chicken Little, how would you have felt when the other animals wouldn't help you?
— If you were Chicken Little, what would you have said when the other animals asked for some of the bread?
— What did Chicken Little teach the other animals?

Rights We Want, But Don't Yet Have
Rights: How to Earn Them:

I Kept an Agreement
A Sharing Circle

Purpose:
To recognize the students for successfully keeping their commitments; to identify the relationship consequences of failing to keep commitments.

Introduce the Topic:
Our topic for this sharing circle is, "I Kept an Agreement." An agreement is like a promise or a commitment — something one person tells another that he or she will do. By keeping an agreement, a person is acting responsibly, which is very important to the relationship between two people. We all know how it feels when someone promises to do something and then doesn't do it. We feel disappointed, and our opinion of that person may even be damaged.

Think of a time when you did what you promised to do. Maybe you agreed to clean your room before dinner, take the dog for a walk, or bring your grade up in reading. Perhaps you promised to come straight home from school and take care of a younger brother or sister while your parent went shopping. Or maybe you committed to attend soccer practice every Thursday afternoon, or read two library books each week. Whatever it was, you did it. Think about it for a few moments. The topic is, "I Kept an Agreement."

Summary Discussion Questions:
1. What happens to relationships when people don't keep their agreements?
2. Is it just as important for children to keep agreements with adults as it is for adults to keep their agreements with children, even little ones? Explain.
3. How do you feel about yourself when you keep an agreement? Why do your feelings about yourself matter?

Topic Variations:
When Someone Kept an Agreement with Me

A Time I Was Acknowledged for Being Responsible

A Responsible Habit I've Developed
A Sharing Circle

Purpose:
To give the students recognition for existing responsible behaviors; to help them realize that responsible habits are developed through repeated practice.

Introduce the Topic:
No matter how responsible we already are, we can always learn more about this important value. It's also important to give ourselves credit for the responsible things we do on a regular basis. Our topic for this sharing circle is, "A Responsible Habit I've Developed."

When we do something again and again it becomes a habit. That's how some of our responsible actions become habits. We do them so often we don't even think about them anymore. Do you have any habits like that? Maybe you brush your teeth every day without being reminded, or put your dirty clothes in a hamper as soon as you take them off. Perhaps you feed and exercise a pet regularly, or make your bed as soon as you get up in the morning. Or maybe you always finish your homework before watching TV. Think it over and tell us about a responsible action that you do regularly. Our topic is, "A Responsible Habit I've Developed."

Summary Discussion Questions:
1. How does having a responsible habit make you feel about yourself?
2. Can you simply decide to develop a habit and then do it? Why or why not?
3. How are habits developed?
4. What responsible habits did you hear about today that you would like to develop, too?

Topic Variations:
I Took a Positive Attitude Toward One of My Responsibilities

A Task I Didn't Like at First, But Do Like Now

An Irresponsible Habit I've Decided to Drop

A Responsible Habit I Plan to Have as an Adult

A Problem I'd Like Help Solving
A Sharing Circle

Purpose:
To provide the students with practice generating alternative solutions to real problems.

Note: This Sharing Circle will take longer than most.

Introduce the Topic:
In this sharing circle we are going to help each other solve problems —something that is very interesting to most people. It feels good to think hard about someone's problem and come up with ideas for solving it. It also feels good to hear other peoples' ideas, and to know that they care enough to offer suggestions. Our topic is: "A Problem I'd Like Help Solving"

Think about this for a few moments. Decide on a problem that you don't mind discussing, and describe it to us. If other people are part of the problem, please don't say their names. When it's your turn, just tell us what the problem is and how it makes you feel. Then call on those of us who raise our hands. We will give ideas that might help you solve your problem. When you hear our ideas, just listen. Later, if you want to talk more to someone about an idea, you can do that. For now, we will just offer suggestions, with no long discussions, okay? Our topic is, "A Problem I'd Like Help Solving"

Summary Discussion Questions:
1. How do you feel when offering help to someone who has asked for help?
2. How do you feel knowing that people have listened to your problem and want to help you solve it?
3. In what ways have we acted responsibly in this Sharing Circle?

Topic Variations:
Someone Who Helped Me Handle a Problem When I Was Younger

I Helped Someone Solve His/Her Problem"

"I Saw Someone Handle a Problem Very Well

I Made a Mistake and Admitted It
A Sharing Circle

Purpose:
To encourage the students to articulate the importance of being accountable, and of accepting responsibility for their decisions and actions.

Introduce the Topic:
Our topic for this session is, "I Made a Mistake and Admitted It." All of us make mistakes — big, medium, and little ones. Part of being a responsible person is owning up to our mistakes and accepting the consequences, whatever those may be. But admitting a mistake takes courage sometimes, particularly when we really goof up.

Think of a time when you made a mistake and accepted responsibility for it. I could have been either an accidental mistake or a conscious decision that turned out to be a mistake. For example, maybe you forgot to lock up your bike one day and it was stolen. You could have pretended that the thief cut through the chain, but instead you admitted your mistake. Perhaps some friends came over for several hours when your parents weren't home, which was against the rules, and the house got messed up or something was broken. Or maybe you accidentally left the gate ajar and your dog got out. Have you ever lost an important file on the computer, or read the wrong chapter, or messed up a project by gluing a picture down on the wrong page? Whatever it was, instead of pretending to be innocent, you admitted that you had done the wrong thing. Think about it for a few moments. Describe to us what happened to you and others as a result of your mistake, how you felt about it, and what made you decide to tell the truth. The topic is, "I Made a Mistake and Admitted It."

Summary Discussion Questions:
1. How did the other people involved seem to feel about you when you admitted your mistake? How did you feel about yourself?
2. Why is it important to accept responsibility for our mistakes?
3. When you make a mistake and other people are affected by your actions, what responsibility do you have to those people? What can you say or do?

Topic Variations:
I Made a Mistake and Denied (or Concealed) It

I Got Blamed for A Mistake I Didn't Make

I Made a Decision and It Turned Out Badly

I Thought It Over, and Decided Not to Do It
A Sharing Circle

Purpose:
To discuss the importance of exercising self-control; to describe how rational decisions are made.

Introduce the Topic:
Our topic today has to do with making decisions. It is, "I Thought It Over and Decided Not to Do It." Recall a time when you were considering doing something that you had doubts about. Perhaps it involved taking a risk, or breaking a rule, or doing something hurtful. You may have been right on the verge of going ahead with this action, but at the last moment decided against it. Maybe some friends invited you to go somewhere and you really wanted to go, but had a lot of homework to finish. A big part of you was ready to forget the homework, but thinking it over allowed you to make a responsible decision. Perhaps you were tempted to cheat on a test once — someone offered you the answers and it would have been pretty easy. However, when you thought about it, you decided that cheating was wrong and that you should do your best on your own. Have you ever turned down a cigarette, alcohol or another drug after thinking it over? Have you ever been tempted to lie, but decided to tell the truth? Too often, we rush into things without thinking. Tell us about one time when your brain take over and helped you do the right thing. Our topic is, "I Thought It Over and Decided Not to Do It."

Summary Discussion Questions:
1. Where did you find the self-control to stop yourself and think through the situation you described?
2. What causes us to act impulsively, without thinking?
3. How do we learn self-control?
4. What process does your mind go through when you make a decision?

Topic Variations:
I Acted Impulsively and Regretted It Later

A Time I Really Controlled Myself

A Time I Had Trouble Making a Decision

Justice and Fairness

At school, models of justice and fairness are everywhere. Students know whether or not grades are geared to merit and performance. They soon learn which authority figures make judgments impartially, based on evidence, and which are swayed by personal feelings and prejudices. They know who will listen and who will not.

Components of justice and fairness include impartiality in decision making, commitment to equity and equality, openness to information and ideas, use of reason, adherence to due process, and consistent, impartial application of rules, rewards, and consequences.

Specific ways to instill the value of justice and fairness include:

- Create and enforce rules democratically and use infractions of rules as opportunities to foster moral reasoning. Ask: "Do you know what rule you broke?" "Can you explain why the class agreed on this rule?" "Why was what you did wrong?"

- Encourage moral reflection in conjunction with reading assignments, and through writing and discussion.

- Teach the skills of conflict resolution and motivate students to commit to solving conflicts in fair, nonviolent ways.

- When moral issues present themselves, ask the students to weigh the justice and fairness of alternative courses of action.

- Make sure your discipline policy supports the development of strong moral values in students.

- To check the fairness of decisions, have students apply tests of reversibility and universalizability. Ask them:
—*Would you expect to receive this kind of treatment in a similar situation and would you consider it fair?* (reversibility)
—*Would you want all persons to be treated like this in similar situations?* (universalizability)

...And Justice for All
Discussion and Art

Purpose:
To understand the meaning of justice and to find examples of justice in real life.

Materials:
newspapers, white construction paper, colored markers, and pencils or paints

Procedure:
Begin by reminding the students of the last phrase of the "Pledge of Allegiance" which says, "with liberty and justice for all." Ask the students if they know the meaning of word *justice*. Allow volunteers to share their knowledge and perceptions of what justice is. Explain that justice means that everyone gets equal treatment under the laws of our country. It means giving deserved rewards and punishments impartially. It also means not favoring one person over another or showing prejudice against a person. On a personal level, it means treating people fairly and without prejudice or favoritism. It means respecting each other's differences and acting reasonably toward one another.

Give examples of justice at home, in the classroom, in the community, and in the nation. Share some examples from newspaper articles, and offer some personal examples as well, such as:
- All the children at home must do their chores before watching TV or going outside to play. No one is favored.
- Everyone gets a turn to talk when there is a class discussion.
- If an adult runs a red light while driving a car, that person is breaking the law and, no matter who s/he is, will have to pay a fine if caught.
- Everyone in our country who is accused of committing a crime is entitled to a fair trial.

Distribute art supplies and ask the students to think of an example of justice at home, at school, in the community, or in the nation. Invite the students to draw a picture of that example of justice. Under the picture, have them write the words. "This is an example of justice because..." completing the sentence with a brief explanation of how the picture depicts an example of justice. For example, a student might draw a picture of a child holding up a test with an "A" on it, writing below: "This is an example of justice because an 'A' is earned only by people who get a high score."

When the pictures are finished, invite the students to show them to the class, reading aloud the reason why each is an example of justice. Post the pictures on a bulletin board in the class or in a highly visible location elsewhere in the school. Summarize the activity by asking some thinking questions and facilitating discussion.

Discussion Questions:
1. What would it be like if the teacher gave good grades only to his/her favorite students and not to everyone who earned them?
2. Why is it so difficult for us to treat each other fairly?
3. What does it mean to be partial?
4. When is it okay to be partial to someone or something? When is it not okay?
5. What is the difference between being partial and being prejudiced?
6. A popular saying states that "justice is blind." What does that mean? Do you think justice in our country is really blind?

An Open Mind
Stereotyping in Literature

Purpose:
To learn about problems created by stereotyping people; to empathize with the feelings experienced by victims of stereotyping.

Materials:
examples from literature that deal with problems related to stereotyping (see "Procedure"); unlined paper and pencils or markers

Procedure:
Begin this activity by discussing the meaning of the word *stereotype*. Ask if any students know what it means to stereotype another person, or if they can give an example of stereotyping. If necessary, give the students a definition and provide examples yourself. In your own words, explain:

To stereotype means to have a fixed idea about a particular group of people and to judge all members of the group according to that idea. Stereotyping means making assumptions about people based on little knowledge. For example, some people think that girls are afraid of bugs and snakes. They don't look at the individual girl and decide whether or not she is afraid. Other people think that boys can't play with dolls because dolls are for girls. They don't consider that a boy might be pretending to be "Daddy" while holding a doll. Another example involves ideas some individuals have about rich people and poor people. They think that all rich people are snobs and all poor people are lazy. These assumptions stereotype people. Stereotyping leads to prejudice, which involves judging people or treating them badly because of a belief about them that is usually wrong to begin with.

Share with the students any incidents of stereotyping and prejudice that have occurred in your life or the life of someone you know. Think of examples related to academic ability (*nerd* or *dummy*), gender (*stupid girl* or *awkward boy*), athletic ability (*jock* or *klutz*), color of hair (*dumb blonde*), race (*stupid, lazy, greedy, cheap*), economic status (*poor white trash*), or religion (*ugly names given to members of a religious group*). Ask the students how they would feel if someone said something untrue about them because of stereotyping.

Read aloud a story from literature in which stereotyping takes place. Mary Hoffman's, *Amazing Grace* or Dr. Seuss' *The Sneeches* are good ones to use with most students. Paul Pitt's *Racing the Sun*, Theodore Taylor's, *The Cay*, or Elizabeth George Speare's *Witch of Blackbird Pond* are possible choices for the upper grades. (See "Justice and Fairness" in the Literature Connection for more selections.) When you complete any portion of the book in which a character is stereotyped, stop reading and distribute unlined paper. In your own words, explain:

This activity is called "Open Mind." I want you to draw pictures and words to show what you think is going on inside the mind of one of the book characters. First, draw a large outline of a head on your paper. Choose one character from the passage I just read in the book. Write the name of that character on the bottom of the paper, under the outline of the head. Next, imagine what that character is thinking and feeling during these moments in the story. Inside the outline of the head, draw pictures and symbols and write words to represent the character's thoughts. Put as many pictures, symbols, and words as you like inside the "Open Mind," as long as they represent what you think your chosen character is thinking and feeling.

When everyone is finished, invite the students to share their "Open Minds," explaining the meaning of the pictures, symbols and words. If time permits, repeat the entire process using a new passage from the same story, or from a different story. Conclude the activity by asking questions to stimulate discussion.

Discussion Questions:

1. What would you like others to know and understand about you?
2. How can we help prevent people from stereotyping us and others?
3. What are some of the consequences of stereotyping?
4. How does the stereotyper lose by refusing to see people as individuals?

Celebrating Our Differences
Music and Creative Movement

Purpose:
This activity is designed to help the students develop understanding of and respect for individual differences by practicing tolerant behaviors toward each other.

Materials:
chalkboard or whiteboard and writing implements; instrumental musical selections on record, tape or CD; record player, tape recorder or CD player

Procedure:
Begin this activity by asking the students to think about all the ways in which people are the same. Invite volunteers to share their ideas while you list them on the board. Some suggestions might include humanness, basic needs (air, water, food, sleep), ability to communicate, ability to move body parts, and the five senses. Next, ask the students to think of ways in which people are different. The following are possible answers: sex, ages, cultural background, race, language, talents, looks (color of hair, eyes, skin, height, and weight) and disabilities. List these on the board, too. Explain that people are often intolerant of each other's differences and sometimes treat others unfairly because of one or more of these differences. In order to live peacefully together, people must respect each other's differences. In fact, by celebrating differences, people are more apt to enjoy a diverse, joyful, and creative life.

Announce that the students are going to participate in a movement activity in which each person will have an opportunity to creatively express what makes him/her unique and different.

Divide the students into groups of three or four, ensuring a diversity in each group with respect to gender, culture, talents, personalities, size, and any other differences that you feel are important. Ask each group to discuss their differences and think of creative movements that represent each person's unique qualities. Explain:

Be sure to develop several unique movements for each member of your group. The movements should fit the special qualities of the person. Practice a "dance" or "pantomime" in which each person performs his/her representative movements while the other members of the group hold positions that spotlight or support the featured person.

While the groups are creating their movements, play instrumental music that can later be used to accompany the dances. Invite the students to practice to the rhythm of the music. Circulate and give support and suggestions as needed.

Invite each group to perform its completed dance before the entire class. Ask the audience to notice how each individual expressed his/her uniqueness and how group members demonstrated their support. After each performance, discuss these observations. Conclude the activity by asking one or more questions and facilitating a summary discussion.

Discussion Questions:
1. How did it feel to acknowledge and support each other's differences and to have your own differences celebrated?
2. How can celebrating diversity, or people's differences, make the world a more enjoyable place in which to live?
3. What would the school be like if we were all the same? What would our community be like? ...our nation?
4. Why do you think people are afraid of differences? How can such fears be overcome?

The Hot Seat
Character Analysis and Role-Play

Purpose:
To analyze the behaviors, feelings, and motives of characters from literature who are portrayed as bullies or the victims of bullies.

Materials:
Copies of children's books that depict situations in which children exhibit bullying behaviors, e.g., (for primary children) Marc Brown's *Arthur's April Fool*; (grades 3 & 4) Carol Carrick's *What a Wimp!*; and (grades 5 & 6) Mary Stolz's *The Bully of Barkham Street* or Katherine Paterson's *The Great Gilly Hopkins*. See "Literature Connection: Justice and Fairness" for additional suggestions. Puppets or character masks are optional in this activity.

Procedure:
Read aloud to (or with) your class a children's book that features a bully and one or more victims. After reading a passage in which the bully mistreats someone, stop reading and divide the students into small groups of three to five. Ask the groups to brainstorm questions that they would like to ask either the bully or the victim in the story. Instruct the students to focus their questions on *how* the character feels about what happened or *why* the character behaved in a particular way. Tell them that they may also ask questions that directly address the problem. For example, the students might ask each character what s/he would do differently if it were possible to change the events of the story. Direct the groups to think of two questions for each character.

After the groups have generated and recorded their questions, instruct them to quickly go through the questions addressed to each character, and share ideas about how that character might answer. Urge the students to try to think just like the character would think, and to create answers as similar as possible to what the character would say if s/he could be brought to life.

Place three or four chairs in the front of the room, facing the class. Gather the class together and invite volunteers to role-play the characters from the story by sitting in these "hot seats" and answering questions generated by the small groups. Invite the students in the "audience" to ask questions, and direct the players to answer "in character." After each player has answered several questions, allow other students to have a turn on a hot seat.

Conclude the activity by asking several open-ended questions to stimulate discussion.

Discussion Questions:
1. What are some things that you can do when you are being bullied (harassed) by another person?
2. If you observe a bully in action, what can you do to help the victim of the bully?
3. What motivates a bully — what are bullies after?
4. In a just and fair classroom/school, what do you think should be done about bullies?

Adaptations:
In primary classrooms, brainstorm ideas as a class while you act as a scribe, recording all contributions. In classrooms where students are uncomfortable playing the roles of story characters, consider using puppets or character masks to depersonalize the role playing.

Classroom Constitution
Discussion and Voting

Purpose:
To promote moral reasoning and democratic process. To create ownership of rules and a moral obligation to follow them.

Materials:
chalkboard or whiteboard and writing implements; pencils and writing paper

Note: Although this activity is best done at the beginning of the school year, it is also effective during the year as a means of reevaluating classroom rules and assessing the need for new ones.

Procedure:
Introduce this activity by asking the students, "Why do we have rules in school?" Encourage a discussion concerning the purpose of rules. Possible answers might include:
- Rules help keep order.
- Rules help to ensure individual and group safety.
- Rules help create an atmosphere for learning.
- Rules provide guidelines for everyone to follow.

Then, ask the students, "What would school be like if we had no rules?" Expect answers like:
—"Tough kids would always get what they wanted."
—"It would never be quiet enough to learn or get our work done."
—"Everything would be a mess."
—"School wouldn't be any fun."

Distribute paper, and ask each student to list one or two rules that should be followed in the classroom. Explain that the group is going to create a "Classroom Constitution," a set of rules that will help make the classroom a safe, productive, enjoyable place for all. In your own words, elaborate:

Everyone will have an opportunity to contribute ideas for the rules and to vote on five or six rules for the class to agree upon and adopt. Keep in mind that everyone must be treated equally and fairly under the "Classroom Constitution."

When the students have finished their individual rule generation, divide the class into groups of three or four to share and discuss the importance of each person's rule suggestions. Explain that during the sharing it is okay for the students to think of another important rule or to change their minds about one or more of their original rules.

After the small groups have had time to process their rules, gather the whole class together and ask volunteers to state their rules while you write them on the board. List all stated rules, even those that are similar to ones already listed. Then discuss with the students which rules can be combined or which of two or more similar rules is easier to understand. Narrow the list down to rules that are distinctly different from one another. Make sure that as many decisions as possible are made by the group, but feel free to add any rule that *you* need. Tell the students: "I need to have this rule." Finally, have the students vote for the five most important rules they are willing to follow. Do this by a show of hands or by secret ballot.

List the rules on a large sheet of butcher paper under the heading "Classroom Constitution." Under the rules write this statement: "I agree to follow these rules." Then ask the students to sign their names, thereby giving "public notice" of their agreement. Post the "Classroom Constitution" in a highly visible place in the room. In a follow-up discussion, extend thinking to more global issues.

Discussion Questions:
1. How are laws made in our society?
2. Are we obligated to follow the laws of our country? Why?
3. Are all of our laws fair to every citizen? What do you think we can do to change unfair laws?
4. Why do we have penalties for people who break the law?
5. Do you think most people would follow society's laws even if there were no penalties? Why or why not?

Just and Fair Solutions
Class Meeting and Dramatization

Purpose:
To encourage moral thinking in problem-solving situations; to cultivate skills required to resolve conflicts fairly.

Materials:
chalkboard or whiteboard and writing implements; puppets (optional)

Procedure:
The day before you lead this activity, throughout the day, write down any conflicts observed in the classroom or on the playground. These conflicts may involve either your students or students from other classes.

Call a class meeting, and explain that you want to discuss a problem situation that you observed the day before. Write these headings across the top of the board: *Reasons, Feelings, Solutions*. Describe one of the conflicts that you observed. Instead of mentioning names, say "Person #1", "Person #2," etc., or use another way to identify the people involved without giving away their identities. Focus the students on the conflict and the moral issues, not on personalities.

Next, challenge the students to think of possible reasons for the problem. Invite them to discuss the reasons while you list them on the board under the first heading (Reasons). Then, ask the children to imagine how each of the parties in the conflict felt. As feeling words are shared, write them on the board under the second heading (Feelings).

Divide the class into groups of three or four and explain that their task is to brainstorm possible solutions to the conflict that are just and fair. Remind the students that seeking the advice of a responsible adult is an acceptable solution. Allow 5 to 10 minutes for brainstorming.

Ask the groups to choose their best solution and share it with the rest of the class. List alternative solutions on the board under the third heading (Solutions). Be sure to add any alternatives that you believe are important. When all alternatives are listed, discuss the probable consequences of each one. Then invite the students to select the best solution through a show-of-hands vote.

Finally, ask volunteers to role play the conflict, the feelings, and the identified solution. Following the role play, ask the actors and the audience:
—*Would this solution work in real life? Why or why not?*

If the students indicate that the solution is unworkable, discuss what is needed to make it work. Remind the students that some problems have no easy solutions and more than one alternative may have to be tested.

Repeat this activity every day for a week to attune the students to resolving conflicts. After that, hold conflict-resolution meetings as the need arises. Conclude the activity with a summary discussion.

Discussion Questions:
1. If you were involved in a similar conflict, how would you try to resolve it? Would your solution be fair to everyone involved?
2. Why is it important to think of different alternatives, rather than do the first thing that comes to mind?
3. How do you know if an alternative is just or unjust, fair or unfair?
4. What can you do if your solution to a problem doesn't work?

Adaptation:
Some students, especially primary-aged children, may be more comfortable enacting the role play through puppetry. Allow them to enlist puppets to do the acting and talking for them.

A Friend Who Is Different From Me
A Sharing Circle

Purpose:
To acknowledge, accept, and support individual differences.

Introduce the Topic:
Our topic today is, "A Friend Who Is Different From Me." Do you have a friend who is different from you in some way? Maybe the friend is a boy and you are a girl. Or perhaps your friend is better at something than you are, like sports or science. Maybe your friend is of a different race or from a culture that celebrates different holidays. Is your friend much older or younger than you? Why did you decide to be friends? How do you feel about your differences? Do you accept each other's differences, sometimes forgetting that you even have differences? Think about all of the things you and your friend do together. What makes this person a friend? How do you feel about each other? Think of a friend who is different from you in some way. You don't have to give your friend's name when you share, just describe the person and your friendship. Once again, the topic is, "A Friend Who Is Different From Me."

Discussion Questions:
1. Why do we sometimes choose friends who are different from us?
2. What would it be like if all of your friends were just like you in every way?
3. Do you and your friend ever have conflicts because of your differences? If so, how do you resolve them?

Alternate topic:
I Lost a Friend Because I Was Different

A Time Someone Treated Me Unfairly
A Sharing Circle

Purpose:
To think about and understand the effects of unfair treatment.

Introduce the Topic:
Today's Topic is, "A Time Someone Treated Me Unfairly." Has there ever been a time when you felt someone treated you unfairly? Perhaps someone "stereotyped" you. For example, maybe someone said that you couldn't go to a baseball game because you were a girl and baseball was for boys. Or maybe a person called you a name and wouldn't play with you because you spoke another language. Has your parent ever punished you for doing something but failed to punish your brother or sister for doing the same thing? Has a friend ever refused to play with you just because he or she was in a bad mood? How did it feel to be treated unfairly? What did you do? Think of a time that you did not receive fair treatment. The topic is, "A Time Someone Treated Me Unfairly."

Discussion Questions:
1. What do we mean by the words *fair treatment*?
2. Why is it important to treat others fairly?
3. How can we let others know if they are treating us unfairly?
4. How can you stand up for yourself without causing a major conflict? What behaviors work best?

Alternate topic:
A Time I Treated Someone Unfairly.

We Resolved a Conflict by Ourselves
A Sharing Circle

Purpose:
To support just and fair conflict resolutions.

Introduce the Topic:
The topic for today is, "We Resolved a Conflict by Ourselves." Think about a time when you and another person had a problem that turned into a conflict. Instead of making the conflict worse or asking a third person to intervene, you decided to work out the problem together. Maybe you and a brother or sister wanted to watch different TV programs, and were fighting over the remote control. Then you decided to handle the situation fairly by flipping a coin. The person who won the toss got to choose the program that day, and the next day the other person got to choose.

Perhaps you were playing "Four-Square" on the playground and someone said that your shot touched the line and you thought it didn't. Did you both decide that the fairest thing to do was take the turn over again? Have you and another person ever fought over a new pencil that you both claimed was yours from home? Did you decide to share the pencil a half-day at a time until it was used up? How did you feel about the decision? Was it a difficult decision to make? Was it better than having someone else resolve the conflict for you? Think about a time when you and another person had a conflict but decided to resolve it fairly between you. You don't have to mention names. Just describe the incident and how you worked it out. The topic is, "We Resolved a Conflict by Ourselves."

Discussion Questions:
1. When is it is better to resolve a conflict by yourselves rather than having someone else intervene?
2. When might it be best to ask an adult or other responsible person to help you resolve a conflict?
3. What kinds of skills do you need to be a good manager of conflict? How can you acquire those skills?

Alternate topic:
We Tried to Resolve a Conflict, But It Didn't Work

A Time I Listened Well to Someone I Disagreed With
A Sharing Circle

Purpose:
To recognize that being fair involves listening to opposing points of view; to describe what it is like to listen and be listened to.

Introduce the Topic:
Today we're going to talk about being fair to others by simply listening to them. The topic is, "I Listened Well to Someone I Disagreed With." Have you ever noticed that when people are talking, and they reach a point where they disagree, they often stop listening to each other? They may both talk at the same time, or argue, or interrupt each other, but they seldom listen and really try to understand the other person's point of view. Can you think of a time when you had a disagreement with someone but made it a point to listen to that person's ideas?

Maybe you and a classmate disagreed over how to solve a math problem or carry out a project, and you listened carefully to his or her opinion. Perhaps you disagreed with a family member over whose responsibility it was to complete a certain chore, but instead of getting angry, you listened. Or maybe you and a friend disagreed about how to spend a Saturday afternoon, and you gave your friend a chance to explain his or her ideas. Tell us what happened and why you decided to listen. The topic is, "I Listened Well to Someone I Disagreed With."

Summary Discussion Questions:
1. Is it fair or unfair to refuse to listen to someone you disagree with? Why?
2. How do you feel when someone refuses to listen to your ideas?
3. How do we benefit by listening to other people's ideas?
4. Why is fairness toward others a value worth keeping?

Topic Variations:
A Time Someone Refused to Listen to Me

Someone I Know Who Is a Good Listener

A Time When Listening Resolved a Conflict

I Made a Decision Based on the Facts
A Sharing Circle

Purpose:
To recognize the importance of making fair decisions; to describe how weighing facts and evidence contributes to making fair decisions.

Introduce the Topic:
Our topic for this session is, "I Made a Decision Based on the Facts." Have you ever been in a situation where you had to decide something and you wanted to be very fair? If you have, then you probably realize that to be fair you have to set aside your own feelings and try to look at facts and information. For instance, maybe you were asked to help choose a new team member for soccer or Little League. You couldn't simply choose the person you liked best; you had to choose the best player. Perhaps you had to decide the winner in some kind of contest. Instead of giving the prize to your best friend, you awarded it to the person who did the best job. Or maybe you had to help settle an argument between two younger children. To make a fair decision, you needed to hear both sides and gather as much information as you could. We all have many opportunities to make fair decisions. Tell us about one that you made. Take a few moments to think about it. The topic is, "I Made a Decision Based on the Facts."

Summary Discussion Questions:
1. How did you feel when you were making a decision in the situation you shared?
2. What makes a decision fair?
3. Why do people make decisions without looking at the facts?
4. If you have to make a decision and don't have enough information, what can you do?

Topic Variations:

I Time I Decided Based on My Feelings

A Time Someone Made an Unfair Decision

I Made a Decision and Regretted It Later

Caring

Kind, compassionate, and generous behaviors arise from caring attitudes that cannot simply be "taught." Children learn to care for others first by being cared for themselves. They also learn to care by accepting custodial and nurturing responsibilities, such as for pets, and by helping others and being positively reinforced for their efforts.

One of the most effective ways for students to learn the value of caring is through participation in formal service programs and projects. An entire class might assume responsibility for making regular visits to a retirement home, doing chores and errands for elderly individuals living near the school, providing a graffiti watch and removal service, or collecting blankets and food for citizens who are homeless.

To derive maximum learning from service projects, treat them as you would any other subject. Prepare students by teaching them the requisite skills, supervise their efforts, provide ongoing motivation and further training, and give them regular opportunities to discuss and write about their experiences.

Additional ways to promote caring attitudes and actions:

- Be a caregiver to your students. Treat them with love and respect, carefully guiding their interactions, reinforcing prosocial behavior, and helping them to resolve conflicts.

- Facilitate students getting to know each other. Encourage them to accept and respect individual differences, to include everyone as an important member of the group, to be sensitive to each other's feelings, to cooperate and collaborate.

- Teach a conflict resolution process and insist that students use it to find peaceful, win-win solutions to interpersonal problems.

- Talk to the students about specific community service projects in which you are involved.

- Always show consideration for others — parents, other teachers, school staff, counselors, and administrators.

- Demonstrate your willingness to go the extra mile for any student who is struggling.

Dare to Care
Dramatizations

Purpose:
In this activity, students think about and discuss ways of caring and practice caring behaviors in a variety of dramatized scenarios.

Materials:
Chalkboard or whiteboard and writing implement; found materials for props (optional)

Procedure:
Explain to the students that there are many ways to demonstrate caring. Ask the students to think about ways in which they can show care and concern for other people, animals, the school, the neighborhood, and the earth in general. Generate a list of words and phrases that describe ways of caring and write them on the board. Here are some suggestions:
helping
volunteering
cheering
inviting
sharing
smiling
petting an animal
acknowledging
thanking
greeting new students
accompanying
hugging
shaking hands
feeding an animal
watering a plant
cleaning up the playground
thinking about your actions and their consequences
treating others fairly
listening
cheering up someone
giving presents
singing to someone
writing to a friend.

Discuss possible role-play situations using one of the words or phrases on the list. For example, the word *volunteering* could generate these scenarios:

A teacher introduces a new student and asks if someone would show her around the school and help her set up her desk during the next recess. A student raises his hand to volunteer and does the job.

A child, noticing that mom is very tired from working all day, volunteers to set the table for dinner and clear the table afterwards.

Discuss the possible actions and dialogue that might take place in each scenario. Then model the role-playing process by choosing volunteers to act out each scenario.

Divide the class into small groups and have each group choose one of the words from the board. Tell the groups to develop two or three scenarios that, when acted out, will effectively demonstrate that caring behavior. Have them assign a group member to each role, and then practice the scenario, making sure that every person has at least one part to play. Ask the students to repeat this procedure for each scenario they develop.

When the groups are finished practicing, invite them to dramatize their scenarios for the rest of the class. After each group is finished, discuss that group's dramatizations before going on to the next group. Ask, "How did these situations demonstrate the value of caring?"

Following all of the dramatizations, facilitate a culminating discussion.

Discussion Questions:
1. Why is it important to act out situations that demonstrate caring?
2. How do you know when a behavior shows caring?
3. What would life be like if no one cared about you? ...if you cared about no one?
4. Is it possible to care about people we don't know? Explain.

Fairy Tales Can Come True
Literature, Drama, and History

Purpose:
By recalling and dramatizing fairy tales, students identify, experience, and discuss a variety of caring behaviors. They further explore the concept of caring by examining historical figures and events.

Materials:
Copies of fairy tales and fables.

Procedure:
Read or tell a fairy tale to the students. A tale such as "Cinderella" has many cultural versions and lends itself well to this activity. Other good ones include, "The Ugly Duckling," "Snow White," or "The Wild Swans." You might also select one of the many Aesop's fables such as "The Lion and the Mouse." After telling the story, identify and discuss the caring behaviors of various characters. Talk about those who risked their lives to help others, like the sister in Andersen's "The Wild Swans." Expand the discussion to include all characters, good and bad alike, and the motives for their actions.

After the discussion, ask volunteers to dramatize the key events in the story. Review the story sequence and allow the students to improvise the dialogue. After the first dramatization, ask a new group of volunteers to dramatize the same story. In the upper grades, divide the class into cooperative groups and give each group a fairy tale or fable to read, discuss, sequence, and dramatize. After a rehearsal, have the groups take turns dramatizing their story in front of the class. Then lead the class in a discussion of the events and character motivations.

When the dramatizations have been completed, extend the concept of caring to actual historical figures and events. Talk about real people who performed caring and courageous deeds. Some examples are:
- Harriet Tubman, who risked her life many times to help her people escape slavery.
- Sequoya, the Cherokee Indian who worked for 12 years to create an alphabet of 86 signs to put the Cherokee language into writing.
- Florence Nightengale, who nursed many people back to health.
- John Muir, who helped to preserve the natural beauty of the land by collaborating in the creation of the National Parks.
- Dr. Martin Luther King, Jr., who lost his life working for the equal rights of all people.
- Peter Zenger, a colonial newspaperman who dared to print the truth about the wrongdoings of a public figure.

Ask the students to share about people they know who have performed caring deeds. Summarize the activity be asking some thought-provoking questions and facilitating discussion.

Discussion Questions:
1. Why do people dedicate or risk their lives for the sake of others?
2. How can you show that you care at home? ...at school? ...in the neighborhood?
3. When we care about someone or something, what are the feelings that we typically experience?
4. How do *we* benefit by caring about an issue? ...an event? ...an individual or group of people?

I Do Care
Mini Project and Journal Writing

Purpose:
This activity raises student awareness of caring feelings and caretaking actions by giving students an opportunity to practice concrete caring behaviors on a daily basis.

Materials:
writing paper or composition books; writing implements

Procedure:
Introduce this activity by asking the students, "What do you care about?" Discuss various things for which the students experience feelings of caring and concern, such as getting good grades, the well-being of family members, having friends, or learning how to read better. Discuss, too, any real threats that cause concern, such as floods, neighborhood crime, or earthquakes. Next, ask the students, "What do you *take care of* on a regular basis?" If the students have difficulty answering, offer suggestions, *e.g.*, pet, plant, younger sibling.

In your own words, explain the assignment:

Everyone is going to choose a "caring project," which will involve taking care of something for the next two weeks. You will keep a journal, writing down the things you do and how you feel about your project. The purpose of the project is to help you become more aware of the importance of caring for things.

Think of something that you can take care of for the next two weeks. It can be a pet that you already have, a plant, some aspect of the environment, or an object such as a bike. You might want to agree to take care of a brother or sister for a certain amount of time each day. Perhaps you'd like to volunteer to take a neighbor's dog for a walk every day. If you choose an object, like a bike, you must do something every day to take care of it. For example, you can wipe it clean, wash it, polish it, oil it, tighten the screws, put air in the tires, and put it in a place out of the weather. If you choose the environment, you can do things like pick up trash from the sidewalks, reuse paper that has writing only on one side, recycle cans or newspapers, or turn off unneeded lights at home. You will have one day to decide on a project and to get permission from a parent or other adult, if necessary.

Give each student a composition book or writing paper. Ask the students to write a sentence or two describing their "caring project." Have them write:

For the next two weeks, I agree to

take care of _____
(name of person, animal, place or object).

I will do this by _____
(list of specific actions).

_____

Next, have the students develop a log for making daily entries describing their caring actions. Have them write the day and date of the project's starting date on the first line, skip two lines, write the day and date of the project's second day on the fourth line, skip two lines, write the day and date of the project's third day on the seventh line, and continue in this manner until two weeks worth of days are recorded.

Instruct the students to write down exactly what they do each day, as well as how they feel about it. Tell them: *Something must be recorded after each date, even if you forget to keep your agreement. Should this happen, explain why you did not complete a caring action and how you feel about having forgotten.*

If you like, keep the journals at school, and allow time each morning for the students to record their activities from the previous day.

At the end of the project, invite the students to share their journal entries with the class. Conclude the activity with a wrap-up discussion.

Discussion Questions:
1. How did you feel when you kept your agreement and followed through? If you forgot, how did you feel about that?
2. What effect did writing about your project daily have on your actions? Was your caretaking better or worse? Why?
3. Why is it important to care for (and take care of) people, places, animals, and things?
4. Do we care more about people and things when we take care of them? Why or why not?

Variation:
Primary children may need to be taught *how* to care for something before assuming responsibility on their own. If this is the case with your students, approach the activity in a more structured way. For example, have everyone do the same project, and complete all actions related to the project at school. For example, have the students germinate plants from seeds. As the plants sprout, teach the students how to care for their plant by giving it just enough water and plenty of light. At the end of the project, have the students make a visual record of their behaviors by drawing a picture to represent each step in the process.

Profile of a Friend
Brainstorming in Cooperative Groups

Purpose:
To identify the characteristics of a friend or caring person.

Materials:
writing paper, pencils, butcher paper, colored markers, and scissors

Procedure:
Introduce this activity by setting a mood in which the students can think about what characterizes a friend. Read a poem or story about friendship, such as "Androcles and the Lion," a fable by Aesop (see literature connection), or read a proverb like, "A True Friend Is the Best Possession," by Benjamin Franklin. You might sing the well-known song, "It's a Small World," made famous at Disneyland, which speaks about world-wide friendships and the common language of smiles, which mean friendship to everyone.

After the warm-up activity, ask the students to begin thinking about what they look for in a friend.

Next, have the students form groups of four to six. Explain the task:

Your job is to come up with ideas about what makes a friend. As you discuss the characteristics of a friend, list words that describe what a friend is like and things that a friend does — a friend's actions or behaviors. Choose one person in your group to record the ideas on a piece of writing paper.

In primary classes, invite upper-grade helpers to record the ideas of each group. If groups have difficulty getting started, make a few suggestions to trigger ideas. Words and phrases might include: *helpful, cooperative, caring, working together, generous, sharing, thoughtful, polite, courteous, kind, loving, sympathetic, compassionate, nice, smiles at me, spends time with me,* and *listens to me.*

When the groups have finished their lists, give each group several colored markers and a piece of butcher paper on which to trace the body of one group member. Have each group select one member to lie down on the paper, and another to trace around the body with a pencil. Have a third group member refine the penciled outline by tracing over it with a colored marker. Have still another member cut out the paper body. Instruct the groups to copy the ideas they listed during discussion onto their body outline with colored markers. If all of the students can write, encourage everyone to take a turn recording several words or phrases. Suggest that the students write large and try to fill the whole body with the characteristics of a friend.

Invite each group to share its completed profile with the class. Post the paper bodies around the classroom or on a bulletin board titled, "What Is a Friend?" Debrief the activity with a discussion.

Discussion Questions:
1. How might your life be different if you had *all* the traits that make up a good friend?
2. How would the world change if everyone demonstrated the characteristics of a friend?
3. What is one characteristic that you would like to acquire? What will you do to acquire it?

Adaptation:
When using this activity with upper graders, consider substituting the words "caring person" for "friend." The objective is for students to become caring toward others in general, even those who are not personal friends. Upper graders do not relate to all classmates as friends.

The Power of Praise
Acknowledging Each Other in Writing

Purpose:
To encourage students to recognize each other's positive attributes and to acknowledge those attributes in writing.

Materials:
small squares of writing paper; pencils; paper lunch bags; crayons or colored markers

Procedure:
Begin this activity by asking the students how they feel when another person compliments them or acknowledges them for doing something well. Ask volunteers to share their feelings. Explain that all people need and want to hear positive things about themselves. Hearing praise from others makes people want to keep doing the things for which other people are praising them. Tell the students that they can encourage and support each other by exchanging positive words of praise on a regular basis.

Tell the students that they are going to have an opportunity to practice giving each other positive acknowledgments so that this behavior can become habitual.

Give each student a paper lunch bag and some crayons or colored markers. Ask each person to print his/her name on the bag in large letters and decorate the bag with crayons or markers. Suggest that the students draw designs, symbols, or pictures that represent something about themselves.

When the bags are decorated, give each student a stack of writing paper equivalent in amount to the number of students in the class. Give the following instructions:

Pass your bag to the person on your right (in front, in back, etc.). When you receive a bag, look at the name on the bag, take the first piece of paper from your stack, and write a note of praise to that person. The note should contain some positive words about the person or his/her accomplishments. No put downs or criticisms are allowed. You do not have to sign your name to the note. When you are finished writing the note, put it in the bag and pass it to the next person. Keep passing the bags until you receive your own bag back, full of positive notes.

Set aside time for the students to read the notes they receive. Invite students to share their most meaningful notes of praise and tell why those notes are especially positive, encouraging, and/or supportive. Ask students to share how they feel about receiving acknowledgments from their peers. Conclude by discussing the importance of verbally acknowledging others and sharing feelings of appreciation.

Discussion Questions:
1. Why is it important for us to acknowledge each other with positive words?
2. How would our lives be different if we supported each other daily with words of praise and acknowledgment?
3. What must you do in order to have something positive to say to each person in class? (Get to know the person; notice what the person does.)

Adaptations:
This activity can be adapted in several ways to suit the ability and maturity of your class. For example, have your students focus on just one person per day. Or lead the entire class through a sequence of note-writing, with everyone addressing to the same person at the same time. Collect each set of notes and "screen out" negative or questionable notes before giving the remainder to the intended recipient. Primary students may appreciate having their positive notes pasted in a construction paper book rather than collected in paper bags.

Who Cares?
Reading the News and Writing Letters

Purpose:
To highlight and acknowledge the good works of others.

Materials:
newspapers, news magazines; videos of television newscasts (optional); writing materials

Procedure:
Share a newspaper account about a person who did something good. Explain that much of what we read in the newspapers or see on television newscasts is negative. We see people breaking the law or doing things to hurt other people. Emphasize that many people do good things that help other people. Refer to the example in your news article or tell about events you know of in which people have performed helpful and caring deeds. Cite examples of people who have helped others in natural disasters such as earthquakes, floods, and hurricanes. Tell about people who have made breakthroughs in the medical field or invented things that helped humanity.

Ask the students to look through newspapers and/or news magazines and cut out articles that feature people who have performed good deeds. Invite the students to look at television newscasts over the next few days and write their own accounts of good works in action. As an alternative, have the students write about caring actions they have seen in the classroom or throughout the school. After the students share their news stories, post the stories on a bulletin board under the heading, "Who Cares in the News?"

After a variety of news stories have been collected and shared, ask the students to choose one person (or group) who performed a caring act and write letters to that person. Invite the students to praise the person for his/her actions and thank the person for contributing to the world, the nation, the community, the school, or the classroom. Address the letters to the individual in care of the newspaper or magazine in which the article was published or the television station from which the news was broadcast.

Conclude the activity with a summary discussion.

Discussion Questions:
1. Why is it important to thank people who perform caring acts?
2. How would the school, community, nation, or world be different if we all did good deeds every day?
3. What would the world be like if no one made the effort to perform good deeds?

Adaptations:
In primary classrooms, read several news events and ask the class to select one. Have the children dictate a class thank-you letter while you record it on large paper. Ask the children to sign their names to the letter. Enclose drawings depicting the students' interpretations of the good deed.

Make this activity a year-long project in which students write notes of praise and thanks each month to people who are doing good deeds.

A Time I Needed Someone and That Person Cared
A Sharing Circle

Purpose:
This circle is designed to help the students become aware of and appreciate people who care about them.

Introduce the Topic:
Our topic today is, "A Time I Needed Someone and That Person Cared." We have all had times in our lives when we've needed someone else — times when we've needed help performing a task, or felt upset or lonely and needed to talk with someone. We really appreciate people showing us they care at times like these.

Think of a time when you needed to have another person care and he or she did. Perhaps you couldn't figure out how to do your math homework and a friend volunteered to help you after school. Maybe you were scared to go to the doctor's and someone gave you a hug and said that he or she understood how you felt. Or maybe this incident happened when you were a new student in a class or school and someone offered to be your friend. How did you react when this person showed that he or she cared? Did you indicate how much you appreciated what the person did? We've all had people in our lives who cared about us. Think of a time that you really needed someone to care about you and that someone did. Our topic is, "A Time I Needed Someone and That Person Cared."

Summary Discussion Questions:
1. What were some of the main ways in which people showed us they cared?
2. How can we let people know that we appreciate their caring actions?
3. Why is it important to let people know that we appreciate their caring?

Topic Variation:
A Time I Needed Someone and No One Cared

A Time I Showed Someone That I Cared
A Sharing Circle

Purpose:
To acknowledge, validate, and support caring behaviors.

Introduce the Topic:
Our topic today is, "A Time I Showed Someone That I Cared." We are all affected by people who care about us. And we have the ability to influence how others feel as well. Think of a time when you showed someone that you cared and it made the person feel good. Have you ever tried to cheer up a friend who was feeling badly? Perhaps you helped a younger brother with his homework or a little sister tie her shoes. Maybe when your parent was tired from working all day, you helped prepare dinner. Or maybe you told a friend that you understood how he or she felt because you'd felt that same way. How did the person react to your caring behavior? How did you feel about what you did? Think of the many times you have shown someone that you cared, and share one example with us. Our topic is, "A Time I Showed Someone That I Cared."

Summary Discussion Questions:
1. How do we affect the world we live in when we show people that we care about them?
2. Why is it important for us to see ourselves as caring people?
3. How do we learn to be caring people?

Topic Variation:
A Time I Could Have Shown That I Cared, But Didn't

One of the Most Caring People I Know

How I Care for the Environment
A Sharing Circle

Purpose:
To identify and acknowledge behaviors that help preserve and protect the environment.

Introduce the Topic:
Today our topic is, "How I Care for the Environment." The environment is the world around us — the entire earth as well as our immediate surroundings. We all want to live and work in beautiful, pleasant surroundings with many natural resources like water, air, and trees. However, when we don't take care of the environment, our surroundings become unpleasant. Think of what you do to care for the environment and help preserve it and keep it clean and beautiful. Do you turn off the water when you are brushing your teeth so that water isn't wasted? Do you pick up trash on the playground or sidewalk when you see it? Maybe you save and recycle soft drink cans. Perhaps you help plant flowers to make your yard look pretty. Do you help save trees by using both sides of a paper before you throw it away? Think of all the things you do to care for your environment and share one of them with us. The topic is, "How I Care for the Environment."

Summary Discussion Questions:
1. Why is it important to care for the environment?
2. What would the environment be like if no one cared for it?
3. Is it fair that people who care about the environment have to undo the damage caused by people who don't care? Is there anything we can do about that?

Alternate Topics:
A Time I Could Have Cared for the Environment, But Didn't

An Environmental Improvement Our Community Needs to Make

I Wanted It All, But Decided to Share
A Sharing Circle

Purpose:
To describe incidents of generosity; to describe how sharing benefits both the giver and the receiver.

Introduce the Topic:
Our topic today is, "I Wanted It All, But Decided to Share." Sometimes there isn't enough of something to go around. When that happens, we have a choice. We either keep it for ourselves and risk disappointing someone, or we divide it up and take less. Think of a time when you confronted this kind of dilemma. Maybe there was only one piece of cake left, and you could have eaten the whole slice, but decided to share it with your brother or sister. Maybe you were sitting on the couch on a cold night, all wrapped up in a blanket, and another family member wanted to get warm under the blanket, too. Have you ever decided to share a toy, a game, paints, or a book, even though you preferred to have it all to yourself?

Sometimes we have to share <u>people</u>. Perhaps you and a friend were having a good time together and a third person came along and wanted to join in. Or the thing you shared might have been credit or appreciation. Have you ever been basking in the glow of praise and appreciation for something you did, and realized that you couldn't have done it without the help of another person? How did you feel when you decided to give that person his or her fair share of credit? There are many ways to think about this topic. When you describe your example, tell us what made you decide to share. The topic is, "I Wanted It All, But Decided to Share."

Summary Discussion Questions:
1. Why is it good to share?
2. How do you feel when you decide to share? How does the other person feel?
3. What would happen at school if everyone — teachers, students, the principal, all of us — refused to share for a whole day?

Topic Variations:
A Time Someone Shared With Me

A Time I Was Selfish and Felt Bad

I Time I Took Turns

What It Means to Live By the Golden Rule
A Sharing Circle

Purpose:
To help students learn to judge the effects of their actions; to understand and apply the Golden Rule.

Introduce the Topic:
Our topic today is one that calls for an opinion, so you'll want to think it through carefully. It is, "What It Means to Live By the Golden Rule." The Golden Rule says "Do unto others what you would have them do unto you." or "Treat others like you want to be treated." If you always followed that rule, what would your life be like? What effect would the Golden Rule have on your behavior?

How would you act at home toward your family? How would you treat people here at school? How would the Golden Rule affect the things you say to and about others? Imagine yourself following this rule all the time, and tell us what you think it would be like. The topic is, "What It Means to Live By the Golden Rule."

Summary Discussion Questions:
1. How difficult would it be to follow the Golden Rule all the time? How would it feel?
2. Does living by the Golden Rule affect your thoughts, or just your actions?
3. What would life be like if everyone followed the Golden Rule at home? ...at school? ...in the community? ...in the world?

Topic Variations:

A Time I Didn't Say Something Because I Knew It Would Be Hurtful

I Said Something Nice to Cheer Up a Friend

Citizenship

Children can learn the value of citizenship by experiencing the impact of their individual efforts in the close knit community of the classroom and in the larger school community. They can learn that they *do* make a difference when they follow a rule, voice their opinion, vote, properly dispose of trash, work and play cooperatively with other students, listen and stay informed, do their part to make special events successful, respect authority, perform voluntary school service, and keep their parents involved by taking home notices and inviting participation.

When meaningful civic values help define a child's relationship to his/her immediate environment, those values can logically and developmentally be extended to the community, the nation, and the world.

Methods of fostering good citizenship include:

- Teach civic values through academic subjects, the news, TV, and literature. Examine the actions of real people and give them citizenship "grades."

- Find ways of connecting civic values to home and community.

- Display photos and portraits of noteworthy citizens, as well as posters and quotations that reflect the virtues of good citizenship.

- Teach a process for democratic problem solving that includes consideration for all points of view, discussion, debate, and consensus seeking or voting.

- Involve students in decision making and encourage them to share responsibility for making the classroom a positive place to learn.

- Hold regular class meetings to discuss issues and problems that arise, such as disruptive behavior, stealing, social cliques, and hurtful language.

- Involve the students in the creation and enforcement of rules, and in decisions regarding the consequences of breaking rules.

- Talk about how you work with other teachers, counselors, administrators, parents, and board members to determine the policies of the school, and illustrate for students how their needs, wishes, and requests impact the governing of the school.

- During election campaigns, talk with your students about voting. Show voter registration cards and sample ballots. When elections are over, explain who won and by how many votes. Cover local as well as national elections, helping students to recognize that individual votes make a difference.

Playing by the Rules
Understanding the Purpose of Rules and Laws

Purpose:
To create a game using miscellaneous materials and teach it to the class; to describe the rules of the game in writing; to explain how rules and laws help people live and work together effectively.

Materials:
four to six boxes, each containing several small objects, (whistles, balls, sticks, shoes, tools, etc.); writing materials

Procedure:
Introduce the activity by asking the students to think of some games that they like to play. Pick two or three games and talk about those games in some depth. Choose athletic games that are played one-to-one (tennis, badminton) or in teams (softball, soccer, basketball), board games (chess, Monopoly), and other indoor games (Scrabble, Trivial Pursuits). Discuss how the games are played, focusing in particular on rules. Make the following points, jotting notes on the board:

- Rules ensure an even start, safety, and adherence to certain agreed-upon behaviors throughout the game.
- Rules protect both the players and the object of the game.
- To play any game well, you have to know the rules, play as skillfully as you can, and respect the rights of your opponent.
- In some games, points are lost by making fouls. Too many fouls can disqualify a player from the game.
- Fouls occur when you break the rules of the game, either accidentally or intentionally.
- Fouls are behaviors that are not allowed because they create an unfair advantage, are disrespectful or dangerous, or destroy the object of the game.

Divide the students into groups of four to six. Distribute the boxes of objects and writing materials. Then explain:

Look at the objects in your box. Your task is to create a game using some or all of those objects. Decide what rules are necessary in order for the game to work. How are points won and lost? Do fouls occur when certain rules are broken? What is the penalty for breaking a rule? Give your game a name, and have a scribe write down the rules. Be prepared to teach the game to the rest of the class, explaining the rules that govern it.

Circulate while the students are working. Offer ideas and suggestions as needed.

Have the groups take turns teaching their games and rules to the rest of the class. If possible, play each game for a short period of time. (You may need to spread this portion of the activity over several days.)

After each game, lead a short discussion. As you debrief the game, develop an analogy between playing successfully (by the rules) and living life successfully, as a law-abiding citizen.

Discussion Questions:
1. Would any other rules help make this game more fun?
2. Were any of the rules unnecessary?
3. Should any of the rules be changed?
4. Why do we need rules?
5. How are the rules that must be followed in a game similar to the rules you that must be followed at school? How are they similar to the laws of the community? ...the nation?
6. What would happen if we didn't have rules and laws?
7. Who makes rules at school? ...at home?
8. Who makes the laws of our community? ...our nation?
9. Are all rules and laws good? How can we tell when a rule or law isn't fair or isn't working well?
10. When laws are unjust or don't work well, can they be challenged or changed? How?

Adaptation:
If you are working with primary-age children, create a simple game with the entire group. Write the rules of the game on the board or chart paper, then have a group of volunteers play the game. Change any rules that need improvement before testing the game again with new volunteers. Over the course of several days or weeks, create three or four games in this manner, always taking time to discuss the importance of rules not only in games, but in the classroom, at home, and in the community.

Pay to Play!
Investigations, Reports, and Role Plays

Purpose:
To understand that citizens at all levels are obliged to pay a price for the privileges of belonging to a civilized society.

Materials:
access to resources (materials and/or well-informed people) with information about federal and state income taxes, taxes on the sale of various goods, including gasoline and cigarettes, property tax, inheritance tax, license fees, and local/state highway tolls; art materials for visual aids

Procedure:
Begin by asking the students what they have to do when they are outside of a theatre, a concert, or an amusement park ride and want to get inside. When the students respond that they have to pay the price of admission, explain the fundamental idea underlying this activity as follows:

In order to participate, you have to pay the amount of money currently being charged. You have to "pay to play." You might not realize it, but just to live here and be a part of this society, citizens must pay a price. This is true of every civilized country in the world. The primary cost of belonging is called tax, and there are many different kinds of taxes. Only adults pay some types of taxes, and other types are paid by everyone. Money collected through taxes is used to buy things that benefit society, like roads, schools, and police and fire protection.

In addition to paying taxes, citizens are also required to buy licenses for certain activities. All vehicles on the highways must be licensed. So must all drivers. In most areas, people must have a license to keep a dog. Hunting and fishing require licenses, too.

Explain that the students are going to form teams to investigate the collection and use of various taxes, tolls, and license fees. Each team will develop a plan for gathering information, preparing a report, and then giving the report to the class. Stress that the teams can teach their information in a variety of ways. For example, the students may use illustrations, charts or lists, and dramatizations.

Have the students form teams of three or four. Allow each team to choose a topic, avoiding duplications. Topics should relate to the collection and use of funds through these and other sources:
- Federal Income Tax
- State Income Tax
- State Sales Tax
- Inheritance Tax
- Property Tax
- Unemployment Funds
- Disability Funds
- Gasoline Taxes
- Cigarette Taxes
- County (or State) Tolls
- Vehicle Registration Fees
- Driver's Licenses
- Pet Licenses

Distribute any resource materials you may have on hand. Provide guidelines concerning where the teams can go for additional information. In addition to reading, urge the teams to interview adults about the tax, license, fund, or toll they are investigating. Provide names and phone numbers of public agencies where information may be obtained. Let the students know how many opportunities they will have to meet during class to develop their reports, and when the completed reports are due.

Be on hand to assist the teams during their meetings, and to help them over any rough spots they may encounter. At times, clarify the scope of each team's investigation.

On the day of the reports, help each team convey its information as effectively as possible. Allow the class to ask questions, and acknowledge each team for its work. Follow up each report by posing a math problem or two. For example: *Since the sales tax in our state is 5%, how much tax would you pay for something that costs $25.00?*

Conclude the activity with discussion.

Discussion Questions:
1. It is said that we live in a free country. Does that mean we get to live in our civilized society for free?
2. Who pays to live here?
3. In what ways do we pay to live here?
4. What are some of the things we get for our money?
5. What about the leaders of our city, county, state and country? What price do they pay?

Adaptations:
If you are working with primary-age students, narrow your focus to the school itself. Explain that homeowners, businesses and members of the work force write checks to the state when they pay their state taxes. The state then sends the money to the school district which in turn writes checks to pay teachers, counselors, principals, and other staff, and to buy books, computers, food, and all other supplies and services. Allow the children to volunteer for a dramatic scenario in which the following roles are played: taxpayers who write checks and mail them; a state tax collector; a state official who pays the school district; an official in the school district who pays the teachers, custodians, secretaries, book suppliers, etc. To take the dramatization full circle, have several students play business owners and service providers (doctors, lawyers, mechanics, etc.). Have the school personnel buy things from these taxpayers, who then return a percentage of the money to the government.

On Trial
Interviews and Triad Discussions

Purpose:
By interviewing adults and sharing insights gained from these interviews, the students develop awareness of how this nation's justice system works.

Materials:
writing materials

Procedure:
Intrigue the children by telling them about a trial you were involved in as a juror, witness, or observer. (The best example will be one that is not complex, but straightforward, and does not involve a heinous crime.) Tell the students about the proceedings, verdict, and whether or not the verdict was just in your opinion. Then ask:

Have you ever watched a real trial or a television program about a trial? If so, you know how interesting trials can be. The jury and the judge try to do the right thing, but it isn't always easy.

Announce that the students are going to have a chance to interview an adult who participated in a trial as a juror, witness or observer. Explain that their task is to find out what happened during the trial. Afterwards, they will share what they learned in small groups. Reassure the students that they will probably not have to look far to find a person to interview. Suggest that they check with family members, neighbors, and friends first, and, if necessary, request that those people ask co-workers and other acquaintances.

Provide time parameters. Then ask the students to help you brainstorm questions to ask the interviewees. After brainstorming, involve the students in evaluating the questions, choosing the best ones, and putting them in a logical order. Have the students copy the list. Here is a sample:

Interview Questions

1. What was the court case about?

2. Was there a jury?

3. If the case involved a jury, who was on trial and what were the charges?

4. If there was no jury, who were the opposing parties and what were they claiming?

5. What did the witnesses say?

6. What was the outcome?

7. Do you think the outcome was just?

When the students have completed their interviews, direct them to meet in triads and share their findings. Give each child 3 minutes to describe and summarize the trial to the other two triad members. Call time after each 3-minute interval.

Finally, conduct a "listening check." Have each triad member take 1 minute to verbally summarize (reflect) the report of one other person in the triad. Conclude with a class discussion.

Discussion Questions:
1. Why do people serve as witnesses and jurors in court cases?
2. What are the judge's responsibilities during a trial?
3. Why are opposing parties usually represented by lawyers? What are the responsibilities of lawyers?
4. What kind of agreement does a jury have to come to? (unanimous agreement) Why?

The Ones Who Spoke Up
Research and Dramatic Presentations

Purpose:
By playing the parts of famous and ordinary people who stood up for what they believed was right or pursued a seemingly impossible goal, the students gain insight into the courage required to make a public stand.

Materials:
the names of famous and ordinary people, partnerships, and groups written on self-stick labels and placed in a container (suggestions below); writing materials; costumes and props (optional)

Procedure:
Prior to leading this activity, prepare a collection of identification labels and place them in a container. Choose from the following suggestions and/or select the names of individuals and groups relevant to a current (or recent) unit of study.

Famous Individuals:
George Washington
Thomas Jefferson
Abraham Lincoln
Harriet Tubman
Carrie Nation
Susan B. Anthony
Franklin D. Roosevelt
Eleanor Roosevelt
Mahatma Ghandi
Martin Luther King Jr.
Cesar Chavez
Jesse Jackson
Bella Abzug
Norman Rader
Mikhail Gorbachev
Nelson Mandela

Famous Partnerships:
Lewis and Clark
Orville and Wilbur Wright
Jimmy and Rosalind Carter

Issues Debated by Ordinary Citizens and Groups:
- English rule prior to the American Revolution
- Treatment of Indians and slaves
- Women not being allowed to vote
- Annihilation of the buffalo
- Child labor
- Railroads built across the lands of Indians and farmers
- Factory owners recruiting immigrants with false promises
- The fairness of the idea, "separate, but equal"
- Treatment of laborers prior to the formation of unions
- The injustice of Japanese internment camps during W.W.II

Groups Acting for a Cause
(3 or 4 labels for each):
- Participants in the "Boston Tea Party"
- Soldiers in America's wars
- Freedom Riders
- Modern environmentalists

Tell the students that you are going to act out the part of a famous person who had something important to say and do — someone who is well remembered for the courage demonstrated in speaking out. Ask the students to see if they can identify the person you are pretending to be. Develop a context around the character by delivering a short speech stating your character's position and by specifying the location and date of the incident you are depicting.

Ask the students to guess whom you are portraying. If no one guesses correctly, disclose the identity of the person and discuss with the students his/her cause and courage in some detail.

Show the students the container of labels and explain the assignment:

You will have a chance to draw a label from this container. Some of the people whose names are on the labels are famous and some are not. Some labels list issues that ordinary citizens debated openly and courageously, sometimes for many years. Other labels list the names of well known partnerships and groups. If you draw this last type of label, take a few moments to locate the others members of your group before beginning work.

Your task is to act out the part of the individual whose name (partnership, group, or issue description) you draw. Gather as much information as you need to represent your character well. If you are a member of a partnership or group, work cooperatively to complete the research and plan your presentation.

When you make your presentation, tell the class who you are and when you lived (if you are no longer living), and give us enough background information to understand your dramatization.

Have the students draw labels. Provide time for research as well as individual and group planning sessions. Assist, as necessary. Let the students know when their presentations will be made in class.

Facilitate the presentations, ensuring audience understanding by asking questions about context, date, history, etc. Applaud each presentation and urge the class to ask questions of the presenter(s). Direct the presenter(s) to remain in character during the question and answer period. Conclude the activity with a summary discussion.

Discussion Questions:
1. How are our lives today affected by what these people said and did ?
2. Many of these individuals were shunned and degraded, even badly hurt, for taking a stand in public. Why do people risk their safety to speak out?
3. How can we show that we appreciate the good things that have come from what some of these people did?
4. What are some current issues that are causing people to speak out?

Adaptations:
Tell primary children about the American Revolution and the signing of the Declaration of Independence. Show them a copy of the declaration and interpret it so they understand its fundamental intent. Explain how much courage it took for each representative to sign his name to the document and how some of them suffered terrible reprisals for having done so. Point out that if these individuals had backed down, we might still be living under English domination. Re-enact the signing of the declaration by having each child come forward and individually sign the document in the same manner as the original signers did in 1776.

Stand Up and Be Counted!
Conducting Classroom Campaigns

Purpose:
By investigating the issues surrounding a current or recent political race or ballot proposition and conducting a classroom campaign, the students discover how candidates and issues capture the attention and motivation of voters.

Note: The next activity, "How to Make Your Opinion Count," is an excellent follow-up to this activity.

Materials:
information relevant to a ballot proposition or elected office, including statements in sample ballots, articles, and advertisements; art materials for posters, placards, etc.

Procedure:
Announce to the students that they are going to do some campaigning. Guide them in selecting a clear cut, well-publicized current or recent political race or state/local proposition. If any students have strong opinions about the chosen race, allow those students to form a team representing their side; then divide the remaining students between the two teams — one team favoring each candidate or each side of the selected issue. You should end up with two groups of approximately equal size. In your own words, point out:

As this campaign develops, keep an open mind and listen to both sides carefully. Even those of you who feel certain which side you are on now might change your mind at some point. Just listen to the information that the campaign reveals and decide for yourself what (or who) is best.

Provide information (statements in sample ballots, articles, advertisements, etc.) to both groups, and allow them to "caucus" and plan their campaigns. Schedule class time for preparation, demonstrations, and presentations. Provide art materials to students who wish to make posters, placards, hats, and other items for their campaign.

Facilitate campaign demonstrations and presentations in which both groups create excitement and promote their point of view. Encourage the groups to reveal the issues that are most important to their side. After the last campaign event, have the students vote on the issue, or for the candidate of their choice (or conduct the next activity, "How to Make Your Opinion Count!", which includes voting). Tally the votes and announce the winner. If possible, compare classroom results with the actual election outcome. Lead a summary discussion.

Discussion Questions:
1. What did you learn by participating in this campaign?
2. What are the purposes of campaigning?
3. Why is it important for citizens to exercise their right to vote?
4. Many adults who are registered to vote, don't vote. Sometimes as many as half fail to go to the polls. Why do you think that is?

Variation:
Don't wait for election season to conduct this activity. Look at important issues currently being debated before the U.S. Congress, state legislature, or local governing body (city council, county board of supervisors, etc.). Parallel actual events with classroom debates, negotiations, and voting. Have the students compare their results with actual outcomes. Have older students examine media analyses of resulting laws/decisions and their anticipated impact.

How to Make Your Opinion Count!
Debates and Voting

Purpose:
By conducting debates followed by a secret-ballot vote on a specific elected office or political issue, the students experience how elections are won and lost.

Note: The previous activity, "Stand Up and Be Counted!" is an excellent lead-in to this activity.

Materials:
Two podiums for debaters; table and chairs for moderators; ballots and a ballot box

Procedure:
If your class did not complete, "Stand Up and Be Counted!" (previous activity), before proceeding select a recent or current ballot proposition or political race and divide the class into two opposing groups, one representing each side.

Begin by asking the students: *Have you ever listened to a real debate between candidates for an elected office or proponents of opposing sides of a ballot proposition?*

Have each team choose three spokespersons to take turns speaking on behalf of the team's preferred candidate or side of the ballot issue (for or against). Explain that each debater will respond to two questions in front of the class, and that the teams will have a chance to prepare the debaters by brainstorming ideas for their arguments and coaching them to express themselves well.

Have each team develop six questions to ask the debaters (one question per debater). This means that three questions will be posed to members of their own team, who can be coached in advance to answer those questions in certain ways. The other three questions will be asked members of the opposing team, who will have no advance knowledge of the questions.

Announce that, after the debates, the students will hold a classroom election and vote on the candidates or issue. Instruct the students to listen carefully and make up their own minds about how to vote. Urge them to be open to new ideas and information, and to vote as individuals, regardless of which team they are on during the debates.

Place two podiums at the front of the classroom. Place the commentators' table and six chairs in front of and facing the podiums. Guide the debate process, as follows: Two debaters (one from each team) face the commentators. Two commentators (one per team) each direct one question to both debaters, who take turns responding. Next, two new debaters come to the podiums and respond to two new questions from two new commentators. Finally, the last two debaters come to the podiums and respond to the last two questions from the last two commentators.

Following the debates, distribute the ballots and allow the students to mark them and place them in the ballot box. Select an ad-hoc committee with members from both sides to count the ballots under your supervision and announce the outcome.

Bring out the refreshments and allow the students to enjoy a celebration. Encourage impromptu speeches by members of both teams. Winners may revel in their victory and reach out to the losers. Encourage members of the losing team to show good sportsmanship by pledging to support the choice of the majority. Conclude the activity with a brief discussion.

Discussion Questions:
1. Why have a debate before an election?
2. Why is it important for eligible voters to vote?
3. When you are old enough to vote, what will you do to inform yourself about the candidates and issues?
4. What would it be like to live in a country where voting was not allowed?

Adaptations:
Allow primary students to observe debates held by intermediate and upper-grade students. Then allow them to hold their own election. Send a small group of representatives to the class that hosted the debates, and have them announce the outcome of their election.

A Rule or Law I Appreciate
A Sharing Circle

Purpose:
To help the students understand the value of rules and laws; to identify specific rules from which the students experience benefits.

Introduce the Topic:
Our topic for this session is, "A Rule or Law I Appreciate." If it weren't for rules and laws, this would be a very different world — a very hard one to live in. Think for a minute, and see if there isn't one rule or law that you are especially glad we have. For example, you may be particularly pleased that it is against the law for people to take things that don't belong to them. (What if people were allowed to take your belongings just because they liked them?) Or maybe you appreciate traffic laws because they cause you to feel safer when you are a passenger in a car. (Imagine what the roads would be like if people could drive like bumper cars, going wherever they pleased.) Perhaps you're glad that we have a particular school rule, because it makes the school environment safer or more pleasant. Think about it for a few moments. The topic is, "A Rule or Law I Appreciate."

Summary Discussion Questions:
1. If the rules and laws we mentioned didn't exist, what would be the result?
2. What rule or law was mentioned that you did not appreciate before, but do appreciate now, after hearing it discussed?
3. How are rules and laws changed? How are new ones made?

Topic Variations:
A Rule or Law I Would Like to See Changed or Eliminated

A New Rule or Law I Believe We Should Make

I Understand a Rule That I Used to Think Unnecessary

How I Show That I'm a Good School Citizen
A Sharing Circle

Purpose:
To identify and discuss specific behaviors that comprise proactive, responsible citizenship.

Introduce the Topic:
We have two major jobs to do at school. One is to be a good student — to study and learn. The other is to be a contributing member of the school community — a good citizen. In this session, we're going to focus on the job of citizenship. Our topic is, 'How I Show That I'm a Good School Citizen.'

Tell us one way in which you demonstrate that you are a good citizen here at school. Think about the things you do in class and on the playground that help the school community function well. Maybe you make a habit of always following the rules. Perhaps you volunteer for jobs in the classroom, like erasing the board, putting away materials and equipment, or tutoring other kids. Or maybe you participate in a school-wide volunteer group, such as the safety patrol, or the conflict mediation team. Do you always put your trash in a trash receptacle? Do your take home notices and bring back permission slips on time? Do you take part in special events, like assemblies, holiday celebrations, and open house? Think about it for a few moments. Being a good citizen involves many different kinds of attitudes and actions. Our topic is, "How I Show That I'm a Good School Citizen."

Summary Discussion Questions:
1. Why is it important to be a good school citizen?
2. How is being a good citizen of the school similar to being a good citizen of the community? How is it different?
3. Is part of being a good citizen encouraging others to be good citizens? What are some examples?

Topic Variations:
One Thing a Good Citizen Always Does

Something I Can Do to Improve My Neighborhood

A Time I Participated in a School Election

A Time I Volunteered My Services
A Sharing Circle

Purpose:
To help the students distinguish between everyday helpful behaviors and school/community service; to encourage participation in volunteer efforts.

Introduce the Topic:
Our topic today is, "A Time I Volunteered My Services." The idea of "service" is an important one in any community, including our school community. Providing service means lending your help or assistance to a project or effort that goes beyond your own everyday activities. When you volunteer your services, you benefit because the community in which you live (or go to school) benefits.

Think of a time when you volunteered to do something that required you to step outside your everyday life just a little. Maybe you volunteered to help with a clean-up project in your neighborhood or here at school. Perhaps you collected canned foods for needy families or blankets for the homeless. Or maybe you sold candy to raise money for some organization. Have you ever volunteered to help with a special event here at school? Have you ever volunteered to run errands for a sick neighbor? Has your class written letters or made greeting cards for patients in a hospital or nursing home? These are just a few examples of service. Think of something like this that you have done and tell us about it. The topic is, "A Time I Volunteered My Services."

Summary Discussion Questions:
1. Why is it important for citizens to provide service to their community?
2. What would happen if no one were willing to participate in volunteer work?
3. How can you find out about service opportunities here at school? ...in the community?

Topic Variations:
I Gave Something to Help the Needy

Something I Can Do to Improve My Community

A Volunteer Organization I Appreciate

A Change I Would Make to Improve This School
A Sharing Circle

Purpose:
To clarify that changes and improvements are accomplished by interested people working together; to view school and community involvement as civic virtues.

Introduce the Topic:
We all know that nothing is perfect; there is room for improvement in almost every aspect of life. Part of being a good citizen is to work with others to bring about needed change in a lawful and peaceful manner. For today's topic, I'd like you to think about things you would like to see improved here at school. The topic is, "A Change I Would Make to Improve This School."

School is something you are involved in on a daily basis, so you can probably think of a number of changes you would like to make. Your improvement might involve classes, the school building, extracurricular activities, the schedule, breaks, anything at all. Maybe you think we should have more clubs and organizations at school, or perhaps you would like to see the auditorium painted and decorated in a more lively way. Do you think we need more computers? Would you like more business people to visit the school as guest teachers? Do you think we need to stop conflicts on the playground? If you could make one recommendation, what would it be? Think about it. When you are ready to share, the topic is, "A Change I Would Make to Improve This School."

Summary Discussion Questions:
1. What does it take for people to change an institution like this school?
2. Why is getting involved in schools and communities part of being a good citizen?
3. What would happen if everyone was too busy or disinterested to become involved in the school? ...the community? ...the nation?
4. Which of the ideas we discussed for changing the school did you like best? Which has the best chance of becoming reality?

Topic Variations:
A Change I Would Make to Improve This Neighborhood

A Way I Get Involved in School Activities

Moral Reflection

Moral reflection helps students develop the ability to make moral judgments about their own behavior and that of others. As follow-up to the sections dealing with specific moral values, the activities in this unit offer students repeated opportunities to:

1. See the moral dimensions in everyday life situations.
2. Demonstrate understanding of the moral values presented in this book.
3. Practice taking the perspective of others.
4. Exercise their ability to reason morally.
5. Make thoughtful moral decisions concerning typical life situations.
6. Gain self-knowledge by reflecting on their own actions in morally challenging situations.

Throughout these summary activities students are asked to identify the moral values operating in each situation. Permanently displaying a list of the six moral values presented in this book, and their definitions, will facilitate this process.

Ask the students what universal moral values they can identify as playing a role in each story or incident described. Help them identify specific behaviors on the part of people involved that are right, as well as specific behaviors that violate a universal moral value and are therefore wrong.

Encourage students to express their feelings about individual and fictional characters — what they admire, dislike, fear, or would like to emulate.

Stop the reading or action (in the case of role plays) at critical points and ask the students what would be the right thing to do in the situation at that moment. Or ask them to identify what is actually going on in the situation — who is doing what to whom and why. In making decisions about what to do in a situation, insist that the students rely less on gut feelings and more on available information and evidence. Help them evaluate and apply the evidence.

Lead the students in brainstorming alternative actions and solutions. Evaluate each alternative and select one that is both morally sound and effective.

When appropriate, ask the students if they can think of similar incidents in their own lives or the lives of people they know. Ask them to describe what happened in those situations without divulging the names of the people involved. Encourage them to transfer learnings from one situation to another.

Spotlighting Heroes
Activity Variations on a Heroic Theme

Purpose:
To give students ongoing opportunities to observe and experience the moral values and character of real people, past and present.

Materials:
biographies, biographical sketches, encyclopedias, and other resource materials

Procedure:
Moral values are embued with life when students are asked to look at examples set by real people as well as famous (and infamous) fictional characters. Whether studying history or literature, allow your students to be emotionally touched by some characters and repelled by others. Help them stock a personal mental storehouse with moral models. Here are some suggestions:

- Assign students biographies and biographical sketches of various contributors to society (list follows). After reading, have the students choose a means of conveying what they learned to the rest of the class. Possibilities include oral reports, role plays, dance, display art, or directing classmates through a simple simulation game. Encourage the students to work in teams. Occasionally include anti-heroes and villains in the mix, but focus primarily on positive models.

- Have the students identify crucial moments or turning points in the lives of heroes and role play those events. Never leave students with the impression that these moments occur as a result of chance or luck. Emphasize instead the role of individual choice and personal responsibility.

- Every month, display a picture of a hero or heroine and discuss that person's contributions to humanity. Each day, add some new fact about the person, or display and discuss a quotation taken from a published work or biography.

Discussion Questions:
1. What has this person done that you admire and would like to imitate?
2. How did the choices that people made lead to this event or circumstance?
3. What might have happened if this person had chosen a different course of action? What alternatives were there?
4. What was it about the way this person lived his/her life that allowed this great discovery (invention, contribution) to occur?
5. What moral values were especially important in this person's life?

A Sampling of Heroes

Walt Disney
Andrew Carnegie
Arnold Palmer
Abraham Lincoln
Marian Anderson
George Foster
Cicely Tyson
Margaret Chase Smith
Lucille Ball
Franklin D. Roosevelt
Amelia Earhart
Vikki Carr
Thomas Jefferson
Shirley Chishom
Jackie Robinson
Golda Meir
Helen Keller
Bill Cosby
Barbara Jordan
Andrew Carnegie
Joan of Arc
George W. Carver
Marie Sklodowska Curie
Booker T. Washington
Mildred (Babe) Didrikson Zaharias
Chris Evert Lloyd
Pablo Casals
Louis Armstrong
Lee Trevino
Thomas Alva Edison
Richard Buckminster Fuller
Winston Churchill
Louis Braille
Ralph Bunche
Barbara Walters
Mohandas Gandhi
Harriet Tubman
Albert Schweitzer
Martin Luther King Jr.
Raul H. Castro
Jules Verne
Beatrix Potter
Margaret Thatcher
Mikhail Gorbachev
Neil Armstrong
Henry Kissinger
Indira Gandhi
Nelson Mandela
Rudyard Kipling
Eleanor Roosevelt
Sir Edmond Hillary
Dag Hammarskjold
Benjamin Franklin
Henry Ford
Albert Einstein
Charles Dickens
Charles Darwin
Charles Lindbergh
George Washington

Sweet Revenge
A Values Story

Purpose:
To identify the moral values operating in a complex interpersonal situation; to recognize how values guide actions.

Materials:
one copy of the "Sweet Revenge"* for each student (optional)

Procedure:
You may read the story to the students, have them take turns reading, or distribute copies of the story and allow each student to read independently.

Ask the discussion questions, helping the students to identify the values inherent in the story, evaluate the motives and actions of the characters, and consider alternative courses of actions.

*Reprinted from *Caring and Capable Kids*, a book of stories and activities compiled by Linda Kay Williams, Innerchoice Publishing, 1995.

Sweet Revenge
by Thomas Pettepiece

"I dare you," Morey said.

James gulped. Morey had dared him before to do things at school, like ten pull-ups on the high bar, or hijack someone's ball during recess. Once he even dared him to stick out his tongue at the teacher while she wasn't looking, which he did, though he could have sworn she saw him at the last minute when she turned her head and his tongue retreated quickly into hiding.

Never had he felt such conflict. His stomach gurgled like an empty cavern. Beneath him he felt wobbly rubber legs, just like he saw on the Saturday morning cartoon characters. Morey, James, and three other boys were standing right below Mr. Brickle's big picture window, where Mr. Brickle stood every day after school and watched the children walk home. If he saw anyone goofing off, or bothering someone, or worst of all, stepping on his property in the slightest — on any part — the grass or the flower bed with chrysanthemum bulbs waiting for Spring, he would pound on the window and shake his fist at them. And if that didn't work, he would disappear from view for a moment, then reappear on the porch shouting, "You kids better stay out of the yard if you know what's good for you." No one ever really knew what would not be good for them if they didn't, but no one ever had the courage to defy the old man and find out. Until now that is.

All eyes were on James. The growing silence was starting to sound like cowardice in the face of pressure. "Come on James. Are you or aren't you?"

"Yeah. You're the one who's always talking so tough, saying 'Mr. Brickle is as dumb as a pickle,' and stuff like that. Are you going to throw that rock or not?"

James had wanted to for a long time, ever since Brickle had singled him out for parking his bike on the sidewalk in front of Brickle's house. James's dog had gotten loose, and James stopped his bike there so he could chase the mongrel on foot. When he came back the bike was gone. James didn't get it back for a week — not until he went over and apologized to Mr. Brickle, even though his parents said James didn't do anything wrong. The sidewalk was public property, they said. Still, Mr. Brickle or someone else could have tripped trying to go around the bike blocking the walkway.

That night after dinner, James and his buddies had met on the corner of Mr. Brickle's street and decided to get even with the old man by breaking his precious picture window. Then he couldn't stand there and stare at them anymore. Tonight was the perfect time, since, on their way home from school, they'd seen Mr. Brickle's son drive off with him. It was twilight, dark enough so the boys could not be seen crouching in the bushes beneath the window, but light enough that they were able to find the medium-size rock James now held in his hand.

"You're chicken, James," one of them said.

"All talk and no action," said another.

"You've got a yellow streak down your back longer than the highway," Morey blurted out.

"Well, you do it then, Big Mouth," James shot back.

"He didn't take *my* bike, man."

"Yeah, but he's yelled at you as much as me, calling you a punk kid and a juvenile delinquent."

The other boys murmured. It was true. Brickle had insulted them all at one time or another, and not one kid who walked by his house had been spared the wrath of his cruel words. Hadn't Mr. Brickle ever been a kid? What was wrong with him anyway?

"Well, James?" they all echoed in unison. "It's getting dark. Let's go. Now or never."

"Okay, okay. On one condition."

"What?" asked Morey.

""That we're all in this together. If anyone gets caught, we all get caught. And if anyone squeals, the rest will pound him. Got it?"

They all looked at each other for a moment, then back at James.

"Okay. Do it."

James stepped back so he could see the entire front of the house. It was an old wooden house, built over sixty years ago, with brick around the bottom. The section with the big window jutted out toward the street, so while it provided a perfect viewing stand for Mr. Brickle, it also made a perfect target.

James tossed the rock up and down in his palm, higher each time. He eyed the glass as though it were a bullseye on a shooting range. "Let's get Brickle, let's get Brickle," he began to chant. His arm was up in the air now, making circles as if he were preparing to throw the rock all the way to China. "Let's get Brickle," the other boys chanted with him. "Get Brickle, get Brickle, get Brickle," the rhythm continued as the boys spread out so they wouldn't get hit by huge chunks of glass from the enormous window.

"One, two..." James shouted.

"RUN!" cried Morey as they all scattered like squirrels fleeing a hunter.

"Three!"

But James held onto the rock, and then he just let it drop harmlessly to the ground. He turned away just in time to see the other boys disappear around a corner. James had made his decision.

Discussion Questions:
1. What moral values played a part in this story?
2. Did Mr. Brickle show respect for the children who walked by his house? Did he show caring?
3. Did the children show respect for Mr. Brickle? How did they feel about him?
4. Was it right or wrong of Mr. Brickle to take James' bike?
5. Why did James' parents make him apologize to Mr. Brickle?
6. Was it right or wrong of the boys to plot to get even with Mr. Brickle?
7. How could the boys have handled their anger toward Mr. Brickle?
8. What do you think of the other boys for promising to stand by James and then running away instead?
9. Did James fake the other boys out? Did he guess that they would run away?
10. How would you have felt if you were James? What would you have done?

Kids Can Solve Problems
Current Events Research, Brainstorming, and Discussion

Purpose:
In this activity, the students select and summarize current-events articles dealing with important civic issues/events. Focusing on one problem, the students generate alternatives and achieve consensus on a solution to the problem.

Materials:
a news article about an issue or problem that clearly relates to the moral value of citizenship/civic virtue

Procedure:
A day or two before you lead this activity, ask the students to cut a current-events article from a newspaper or news magazine and bring it to school. Require that the articles deal with issues or events of civic importance. Bring an article of your own dealing with a problem for which creative solutions are obviously needed.

Talk to the students about the importance of being well-informed. Explain that the community, the nation, and the world are made up of individuals just like them. Communities are shaped by the interest and participation of individual people working together. People build, produce, feed, govern, and educate. In the process, they create conflicts and problems, which they also must solve. Ask the students what kinds of issues, events, and problems they discovered while reading the newspaper. Ask two or three volunteers to briefly tell the class about their articles.

Then ask all of the students to share their article with a partner. Allow about 5 minutes for this. Finally, read *your* article aloud to the class. Define terms used in the article, and discuss the problem. Ask these questions:
—What is the problem?
—Whose problem is it?
—What moral values are involved in this problem?

Announce that, through group discussion, the students are going to come up with solutions to the problem described in the article that you just read. Have the students form groups of three to five. Give the groups 1 minute to choose a leader and a recorder. Then announce that the groups will have 10 minutes to brainstorm solutions to the problem. If necessary, review the procedure for brainstorming.

Call time after 10 minutes, and have the groups discuss and evaluate their suggestions, one at a time. Their task is to choose one solution to present to the class. Suggest that they answer these questions:
—Will this solution solve the problem?
—Can this solution actually be done?
—Will combining any suggestions make a better solution?

Allow a few more minutes for discussion. Urge the groups to use the process of consensus-seeking to make their decision. Have the group leaders report the class. Then lead a culminating discussion.

Discussion Questions:
1. What was the hardest part about finding a solution to this problem? What was the easiest part?
2. If your group was not able to come to a decision, why not?
3. How were disagreements or conflicts handled in your group?
4. Is there any way for individuals or nations to avoid having problems? Explain.
5. How will learning to solve problems here in the classroom help prepare us to solve them in the outside world?

Adaptations:
If you are teaching primary-age children, conduct the brainstorming session with the entire class, using simple words and symbols to record solutions on the board or chart paper.

The Treasure Box
A Values Story

Purpose:
To identify the moral values operating in a complex interpersonal situation; to recognize how values guide actions.

Materials:
one copy of the "The Treasure Box" * for each student (optional)

Procedure:
You may read the story to the students, have them take turns reading, or distribute copies of the story and allow each student to read independently.

Ask the discussion questions, helping the students to identify the values inherent in the story, evaluate the motives and actions of the characters, and consider alternative courses of actions.

*Reprinted from *Caring and Capable Kids*, a book of stories and activities compiled by Linda Kay Williams, Innerchoice Publishing, 1995.

The Treasure Box
by Dianne Schilling

Cara called it her treasure box, but Susan thought it looked more like a tiny suitcase — soft and leathery with a shiny metal clasp and a fancy carved handle that fell with a "plunk" to one side when Cara set it down.

Every day, Cara brought her treasure box to school and placed it carefully on the corner of her desk. To Susan, the plunk of the handle signaled the start of school as reliably as did the warning bell. Once school started, Cara didn't touch her box again until recess.

Susan slid down in her seat and stared at the box. She thought it looked like the cases that contained expensive chess or backgammon games. But Susan was certain there were no games inside. Games, after all, weren't treasures. Who ever heard of sunken chess sets or buried backgammon? No, reasoned Susan, treasures were made of precious metals and stones — hoarded by monarchs, hid by pirates, and guarded by sharks, and to Susan, no one had ever seemed more suited to such mysteries than pretty, popular Cara.

At recess, Susan observed Cara and her friends escape to the far corner of the playground. She watched them move back and forth along the fence, and huddle close together, talking and laughing — and looking at the contents of Cara's treasure box. But Susan couldn't get close enough to see what the treasures were.

Cara and her friends seldom spoke to Susan. Even when Susan moved to the desk right across the aisle so that she could be closer to the treasure box, Cara didn't notice. And when Susan finally got up the nerve to ask (casually), "What's in the box, Cara?" Cara turned and looked at Susan as though she'd never seen her before. "Things," she said cooly, "Special things."

Susan hadn't really planned to steal the treasure box. It just sort of happened. School was letting out for the day. Kids were sitting on the front lawn waiting for their rides, or running for the bus and for their parents' cars. As usual, the circular driveway in front of the school was jammed. Susan wheeled her bike around the side of the building just in time to see Cara jump up from the grass and run to the curb. Cara leaned over and stuck her head through the open window on the passenger's side of a car and began to talk to whomever was inside.

Walking her bike toward the street, Susan realized that she was going to pass alongside the spot where Cara had been sitting. She saw that Cara's things were still there, stacked neatly in the soft grass. Without missing a step or slowing her bike, Susan reached down and closed her hand around the carved handle of the treasure box and swung it quickly under her jacket. Her heart pounded as she pressed the treasure box to her side. The wheels of her bike hit the pavement with a squeal just inches in front of the car where Cara stood.

Susan maneuvered her way through the idling cars and headed for home. Halfway there, she stopped in a quiet spot and pulled the box out from under her jacket. Pressing firmly on both latch buttons, Susan waited excitedly for the box to snap open. Nothing happened. She grabbed the lid and pulled up on it with all her strength. Still nothing. "Wouldn't you know it!" Susan sighed, transferring the treasure box to her bookpack. "It's locked!"

∼

Susan was an inventor — a collector and an inventor. She liked to invent things out of pieces and parts that she collected from other people's junk piles. Maybe it was the collector inside Susan who wanted Cara's treasure box. And maybe it was because she was always bringing junk home that her family didn't ask where she got the leathery box with the carved handle that appeared that night in her room. Then again — maybe they didn't notice it.

Susan pushed aside papers and equipment and set the treasure box in the middle of her workbench. Susan's father had started to build her a desk a couple of summers before, and she had asked him to make a workbench instead. He had argued that a workbench didn't belong in a bedroom. Susan had argued back that just because her bed was in the room didn't make it a bed-room. It was just her room, and it could be any kind of room. Father had finally agreed, but had insisted on using the oak he had bought for the desk. The completed bench, with its satiny lacquered finish, looked like an oversized, oddly-shaped desk. That seemed to satisfy Father.

Susan waited until dinner was over and the rest of the family had settled into the evening's activities. Father was banging away in the garage on some new piece of furniture. Mother was conducting her telephone interviews and click-clacking the results into the computer. Ross and Michael (Susan's younger brothers) were alternately laughing and arguing in front of the TV. Susan collected an assortment of hand tools from various places around the room and lined them up next to the treasure box. she didn't want to damage the box, so she worked slowly and carefully. She tried one tool and then another.

It took Susan just 5 minutes to spring the latches on the treasure box. She set her tool aside and took a deep breath. Slipping her finger under one of the latches, she slowly lifted the lid.

∽

No familiar "plunk" signaled the start of school the next day. No plunk — and no Cara. When she finally did arrive — sad faced and an hour late — Cara was accompanied by Ms. Estes, the school principal. Mr. Levine stopped his geography lesson and huddled briefly with Ms. Estes, while Cara stood to one side, ignoring the whispers and hand signals of her friends. After what seemed to Susan like an eternity (but was probably no more than 2 minutes), Ms. Estes left the room, turning at the door to give Cara an encouraging little smile. Mr. Levine put his arm around Cara's shoulders and walked her around to the front of his desk till they were both facing the class.

"Most of you have probably noticed Cara's little box — the one she brings to school every day. It was stolen off the grass in front of the school yesterday afternoon," said Mr. Levine seriously. "If anyone knows anything about it, please come and see me — or Cara." Mr. Levine paused. A chorus of sympathetic sounds traveled around the room. Susan looked out the window.

"Cara," continued Mr. Levine. "Would you mind telling the class what was in your box?"

Cara looked hesitantly at Mr. Levine. Then she seemed to fix her gaze on the empty corner of her desk. "Just little things," she said softly. "Nothing important — except to me."

"What little things, Cara?" urged Mr. Levine. "In case someone finds them."

"An old ring that belonged to my grandmother," said Cara. It has fake blue stone in it. A pair of earrings that I bought for when I'm twelve and can have my ears pierced. A couple of notes from my friends. Some poems that I wrote. And pictures..." Cara hesitated, "...of my baby brother mostly."

"No one likes to lose things," said Mr. Levine, "but it's especially sad when the things you lose are very important to you. We all hope you get the box back, Cara."

Cara sat down. Mr. Levine resumed the geography lesson. Susan sketched little boxes in her notebook and waited for recess.

That night, when the TV, the computer, and the furniture shop were once again in operation, Susan left the house unnoticed. She carried a plastic grocery bag. Inside — wrapped securely in an old blanket — was the treasure box. Susan hoped that anyone seeing her would think that she had ridden her bike to the supermarket and was on her way home.

An eight-foot chain-link fence encircled the school. It was always locked at night unless there was a meeting. Susan stood at the edge of the school grounds for a long time, watching for signs of the caretaker. She figured that by now he must be watching TV in his little trailer, but she wanted to be sure.

When at last Susan felt satisfied that the front of the school was deserted, she wheeled around and rode *away* from the school. About halfway down the block, she abruptly made a U-turn and pedaled back toward the circular driveway, picking up speed as she rode. Guiding the bike with her right hand, Susan held the grocery bag at arm's length, the fingers of her left hand clasping its handles together. She began to swing the bag around and around. As she passed the front gate, Susan raised herself high on the peddles and released her grip on the bag, sending it sailing over the fence.

Susan didn't turn around or even look back. She didn't see the bag bounce onto the soft grass. She never knew that it landed only a few feet from the spot where it had rested the previous afternoon.

The treasure box was safe. The caretaker would find it when he unlocked the gate in the morning. He would see the words, "CARA I"M SORRY" lettered largely on the bag. And though the letters would be smeared from the wet grass, he would read them — and he would understand.

Discussion Questions:

1. What moral values did you recognize in this story?
2. Why did Susan Steal the treasure box?
3. Do you think Susan knew that what she was doing was wrong?
4. If Cara had been friendlier to Susan, would it have made a difference?
5. Why do we have rules and laws that forbid us from taking things that do not belong to us?
6. Why do you think Susan returned the treasure box?
7. Susan was able to return the treasure box without getting caught. What do you think about that?
8. Describe the most important thing you learned from the story of Susan, Cara, and the treasure box.

It's a Small World
Group Consensus-Seeking on World Issues

Purpose:
To develop possible solutions to world issues/problems; to take into consideration the moral values involved in each issue.

Materials:
one copy of the worksheet, "World Issues," for each student (page 145); chart paper and markers for each small group; the six moral values listed on chart paper or chalkboard for everyone to see

Procedure:
A day or two prior to leading this activity, distribute and go over the worksheets. Ask the students to complete their worksheet as homework. Remind them that the article they choose must be about a world problem.

Ask the students to help you define the term *issue*. Write their suggestions on the board and interject some of your own. Explain and consider these dictionary components:
—an unsettled matter needing a decision
—a matter of disagreement between two or more parties
—a point of debate or controversy

Have the students take out their homework (completed worksheets). Ask them how well their definition of *issue* fits the news article they chose. Discuss briefly, and then announce that the students are going to work in small groups to develop solutions to one issue per group.

Have the students form groups of four to six and choose a leader and recorder. Distribute the chart paper and markers. Ask the students to take turns summarizing their articles. Suggest that they read from their worksheet, naming countries involved, explaining the issue or problem, stating which moral values they checked and why, and summarizing what has been done about the issue so far. Allow about 5 minutes for this task.

Direct the groups to choose one issue on which to focus. Allow about 3 minutes for discussion and decision making. Ask the recorders to write a statement of the issue/problem at the top of the chart paper. Circulate and assist.

Announce that the groups have 10 minutes to brainstorm alternative decisions or solutions to the selected issue. After you call time, announce that the groups have 10 more minutes to discuss the suggested alternatives. Remind them to consider the moral values involved. Instruct them to cross out ideas that won't work and narrow their list down to the two or three best suggestions.

Have the recorders tape their lists to a wall in front of the class. Have the leaders take turns reporting their group's issue and possible decisions/solutions to the class. Ask the class to join in making a final decision concerning each issue. Lead a follow-up discussion.

Discussion Questions:
1. What was the hardest part about making a decision about your issue? What was the easiest part?
2. If your group was not able to come to a decision, why not?
3. Is your solution an ethical solution? (Is it responsible? ...just? ...fair? ...caring? ...honest?)
4. How were disagreements handled in your group?
5. Is it important for nations to consider moral values when they decide what to do about world issues? Explain.
6. How do nations and world bodies like the U.N. resolve problems?
7. What have you learned from this activity?

Adaptation:
If you are working with primary-age students, omit the worksheet and focus on a school problem. As a total group, brainstorm solutions to the problem. Have the students test each possible solution by answering these (and other) questions:
—Is this an honest solution?
—Is this solution fair to everyone?
—Is this the most responsible thing to do?

World Issues
Current Events Worksheet

Choose a recent article from a newspaper or magazine. The article must be about a world issue or problem. Here are some examples:
—the environment
—world hunger
—trading between nations
—a conflict or war

Read the article and answer these questions:

1. What is the issue or problem described in the article?

_____

_____

2. What countries are involved?

_____

_____

3. What moral values are involved?

___ **Trustworthiness**

Explain: _____

_____

___ **Caring**

Explain: _____

_____

___ **Responsibility**

Explain: _____

_____

___ **Respect**

Explain: _____

_____

___ **Justice and Fairness**

Explain: _____

_____

___ **Citizenship**

Explain: _____

_____

4. What has been done about the issue or problem so far?

_____

_____

5. What suggestions, if any, does the writer make?

_____

_____

5. How do you think the problem should be solved?

_____

_____

_____

Dilemmas by the Dozen
Decisions and Values

Purpose:
To identify moral values underlying the decisions of children and adults in ordinary situations; to recognize how values guide actions.

Materials:
copies of the dilemmas for distribution (optional, depending on method of implementation)

Procedure:
These stories/dilemmas may be used in several ways. Here are three suggestions:

• Occasionally read a dilemma aloud to the students. Ask the discussion questions. Help the students to identify the values inherent in the situation, evaluate the motives and actions of the characters, and consider alternative courses of actions.

• Divide the class into small groups, and give each group a copy of one dilemma (including discussion questions). Have the groups read and discuss their dilemma, answering the questions. Ask each group in turn to summarize its dilemma and conclusions for the rest of the class.

• Divide the class into small groups, and give each group a copy of one dilemma. Have each group develop, rehearse, and deliver a role play of its dilemma for the rest of the class. After each role play, ask the discussion questions, allowing the entire class to respond. Brainstorm alternative actions in each situation and ask the performing group to role play one or two of those.

~

Larry is supposed to meet Paul and Robert for a frisbee game at the park. Just as he is about to leave, he receives a phone call from Manny. Manny is studying for the math test tomorrow and sounds very confused and worried. He asks Larry to come over and help him. Larry and Manny are good friends, so Larry doesn't want to upset Manny, but he doesn't want to miss the game either. He decides to tell Manny that he has to go somewhere with his parents.

The next morning at school, Paul tells Manny that he missed a good frisbee game the previous afternoon, and he mentions that Larry was there. Manny feels hurt and angry. During the math test, he tries to copy off of Larry's paper.

Discussion Questions:
1. What are the moral values in this situation?
2. How would you feel if you were Larry?
3. What could Larry handle the situation?
4. How would you feel if you were Manny?
5. What could Manny do?

~

The Dennis family lives atop a hill at the end of a long, steep winding driveway. The lot is large and tree covered. One evening, when Mr. Dennis pulls up the driveway and parks his car, he forgets to put on the emergency brake. Almost immediately, the car begins to inch backwards toward the slope. During the night it crosses the edge of the driveway, picks up momentum, rolls down the hill and crashes into a tree on the edge of the Henry's yard. The car is a total loss and the Mr. and Mrs. Henry are angry about the tree, which they insist is going to die. Mr. Dennis explains what happened and apologizes. He cleans up the mess and suggests everyone wait to see if the tree recovers. But the Henrys demand to be paid immediately for the damage. Reluctantly, Mrs. Dennis calls the insurance company, which pays Mr. and Mrs Henry $7,000 — the cost to replace the tree with a similar full-grown shade tree. Weeks pass, and the original tree not only recovers — it looks healthier than ever. The Henrys keeps the $7,000 and, when Mr. and Mrs. Dennis renew their insurance policy, they discover that the accident has caused their rates to increase. The two families quit speaking to each other.

Discussion Questions:
1. What are the moral values in this situation?
2. Who is responsible for what?
3. What is right about the way this situation was handled? What is wrong?
3. If you were Mr. and Mrs. Dennis, how would you feel? What would you do?
5. If you were Mr. and Mrs. Henry, how would you feel? What would you do?
4. Did the insurance company do the right thing?

Julie has a plan to create an elaborate science project that she is sure will win the big science-fair prize. She gets started, but quickly runs into problems, so he asks Liz to be her partner. Both are good science students, but Liz is especially good at solving problems and building things. On the day of the science fair, Liz is sick, so Julie sets everything up and demonstrates the project by herself. Sure enough, the project wins first prize. When Julie is interviewed by reporters, she doesn't give any credit to Liz. In fact, she never mentions that she had a partner at all. She answers every question with, "I did this," or "I did that." When Liz sees Julie's picture in the paper and reads the article, she feels bad. But she never says anything to Julie.

Discussion Questions:
1. What are the moral values in this situation?
2. If you were Liz, how would you feel? What would you do?
3. How do you think Julie feels? How *should* she feel? What should she do?
4. What would you like to see happen in this situation?

On Saturday, Ms. Hornaday goes to Lacy's department store and buys $200 worth of holiday gifts for her family and friends. On this shopping day only, the store is offering one $10 gift certificate for every $100 a customer spends. Before leaving the store, Ms. Hornaday shows her receipts to the customer service clerk and receives two gift certificates, which she can use to buy $20 worth of merchandise. Later, at home, Ms. Hornaday decides that some of the gifts were poor choices. The next day, she returns half of the items. The store accepts her returns and refunds her money, but Ms. Hornaday keeps — and plans to use — both gift certificates.

Discussion Questions:
1. What are the moral values in this situation?
2. If you were Ms. Hornaday, what would you do with the gift certificates? Why?

Maria and Colleen are walking home together on a particularly hot afternoon. When they get to Maria's house, Colleen says goodbye and continues down the block. Suddenly, she hears Maria calling after her, "Hey, how about a swim in my pool?" Colleen hesitates. A swim would feel wonderful, but Colleen knows that Maria's parents are both at work. Even Maria isn't supposed to swim unsupervised, let alone a friend of Maria's. They could both get in a lot of trouble.

When Colleen tells Maria about her fears, Maria says, "Don't worry, no one will find out. On a day like this, everything will dry off real fast — including us. Come on!"

Colleen gives in, and the two girls head for the pool. When Colleen gets home, her mother asks why she is late. Colleen says that she stayed after school to help the teacher.

Discussion Questions:
1. What are the moral values in this situation?
2. Why do Maria's parents have a rule against swimming without supervision?
3. What are Maria's responsibilities in this situation? What are Colleen's?

Mr. Escobar takes his car to the garage for a smog test and certificate. The car fails the test and the mechanic tells Mr. Escobar that the necessary repairs will cost $60. Mr. Escobar has heard about a man who will fake a smog certificate for $20. Several of Mr. Escobar's coworkers have gone to this man, rather then have their cars fixed. Mr. Escobar wonders if he should go, too.

Discussion Questions:
1. What are the moral values in this situation?
2. If a lot of people get fake smog certificates, what are the consequences?
3. Who is breaking the law in this situation?
4. What do you think Mr. Escobar should do?
5. Does anyone have a moral obligation to report the man who is faking smog certificates? Who and why?

~

When Mr. and Mrs. Greer go on vacation for three weeks, they ask Kim to feed their cat, Sydney, twice a day. They also ask her to water their yard and houseplants. They offer to pay Kim $10 a week and she agrees. Every morning before school, Kim stops by the Greer house. Sydney is always waiting for his breakfast near the back door. In the evening, she returns, feeds the cat his dinner, and checks to see if anything needs watering. For the first two weeks, Kim sticks to this routine. However, during the third week, Kim herself has vacation from school and sleeps later than usual. On Monday and Tuesday, she doesn't get around to feeding Sydney his breakfast until 10:00 a.m. and forgets to check the plants. On Wednesday, she stops briefly at noon before rushing off to a friend's house. On Thursday, Kim goes to a movie in the evening and forgets to feed the cat his dinner. When she goes over on Friday morning, Sydney isn't at the back door and doesn't answer her call. Friday evening, Sydney is in the yard, but doesn't seem hungry.

When the Greers arrive home on Sunday, they pay Kim and ask how everything went. She tells them, "Fine." On Monday evening, the Greers phone and ask Kim to come next door and answer some questions. They ask Kim why Sydney showed up hungry at another neighbor's house several times during the previous week, and why two of their favorite house plants are dry and wilted. Kim acts surprised and tells them she has no idea why. She insists that she did everything they asked her to do.

Discussion Questions:
1. What are the moral values in this situation?
2. What do Kim's actions say about her?
3. How did Kim's actions affect the cat? ...the plants? ...the Greers? ...Kim?
4. What should Kim have done?

An employer mismanages his company and is frequently late paying his workers. Robert, an employee of the company, decides he's had enough and plans to quit. He tries to collect his back pay before announcing his resignation, but the employer still owes him $2,000. Robert comes up with a plan: Before turning in his key, he will go to the office at night and remove the computer from his desk. The computer, worth about $2,000, does not belong to Robert, but he is the only one who uses it.

Discussion Questions:
1. What are the moral values in this situation?
2. What are the employer's responsibilities?
3. What are Robert's responsibilities?
4. What's wrong with Robert's plan?
5. How would you feel if you were Robert and never knew whether or not you were going to be paid? What would you do?
6. How would you feel if you were the employer and one of your workers left with equipment that belonged to you? What would you do?

Louis heads down the street to see if Jimmy wants to do some skateboarding. He finds his friend in the garage sorting piles of newspapers, cans, and bottles. "That's no fun. Can't you do it later?" urges Louis.

"No," answers Jimmy. "I have to finish getting this stuff ready for Mom and me to take to the recycling center."

"Why don't you just throw it away?" asks Louis. "The trash collector is coming tomorrow."

"Because if we throw it in the trash, it will go to the landfill," answers Jimmy, "and if we take to the recycling center, it won't. It'll be used again. Don't you collect things for recycling at your house?"

"No," shrugs Louis. He unwraps a candy bar and starts eating it.

"Why?" asks Jimmy.

"I don't know. Too much trouble I guess."

Louis heads his skateboard back out to the street. "See you later," he calls, coasting smoothly onto the pavement.

Jimmy looks up from his work just in time to see Louis throw the candy wrapper into the gutter. He opens his mouth to yell, but Louis was already halfway down the block. Jimmy sighs and shakes his head. Then he walks out to the curb and picks up the candy wrapper.

Discussion Questions:
1. What are the moral values in this situation?
2. What do the actions of the two boys say about them?
3. How can people show respect for the environment?

~

Newt doesn't have enough money to pay his rent. After several weeks of unemployment, he has just started a new job and has not been paid yet. The landlord telephones and asks when he can expect a check. Newt plans to move to a cheaper house next month, but is afraid to tell the landlord. He thinks about lying, just to keep the landlord off his back. He figures it will take the landlord a few weeks to evict him, during which time he can save his money for a new place. But the landlord has always been cooperative and nice, and Newt feels guilty taking advantage of him. Newt wonders what will happen if he tells the truth. If the landlord kicks him out, Newt has nowhere to go.

Discussion Questions:
1. What moral values are involved in this situation?
2. How do you think the landlord feels?
3. If you were Newt, how would you feel? What would you do?

On Saturday, Bud and Holly stop by the library to turn in some books and see Mai working alone at a back table. They walk over to say hello.

"What are you working on Mai?" asks Holly.

"I decided to enter the Flag Day essay contest," answers Mai. "The winning essay will be printed in the newspaper. That would be a great honor. Are you going to enter?"

"No," says Holly.

"I haven't given it much thought," responds Bud. "What are you writing about?"

"The meaning of the flag," answers Mai. "It's a little hard because I haven't lived in this country very long. Maybe you can help me. What does it mean to you?"

"I don't know," answers Holly. "But we say a pledge to the flag."

"I haven't given it much thought," responds Bud. "But last year at school, I helped put the flag up and take it down."

"What about liberty and justice?" asks Mai. "Those words are in the pledge. Don't they mean anything to you?"

"Oh, sure they do," shrugs Holly.

"I haven't thought much about it," says Bud. "But this is sure a boring way to spend a Saturday. Why don't you come to the movies with us instead."

Mai thinks for a minute, then smiles and says, "Thank you. But I must write. In the country where I used to live, we didn't always have the liberty to choose what we wanted to do on Saturday. And if there was an essay contest, all students had to enter. They didn't have the liberty to refuse. If they refused, their whole family could be punished. In the United States, I can choose to write — or not to write. I like that. That is liberty and justice."

As Holly and Bud start to leave, Mai calls softly after them, "Thank you for helping me with my essay. You gave me some great ideas."

Discussion Questions:
1. What are the moral values in this situation?
2. If you were Holly or Bud, how would you feel about Mai?
3. What does Mai like about living in the United States?
4. What can Holly and Bud learn from Mai's example?

Kurt enjoys riding his bike to school the morning after a storm. Sometimes he flies fast down the wet streets, sending spray up on all sides. Other times he navigates between the puddles, wheeling this way and that like an infantryman avoiding land mines. This morning, he nearly makes it to school without becoming a casualty. When he loses his traction and goes down a block away, everything gets wet, including the adventure comic book Sergio loaned him the day before. It is soaked and muddy.

Kurt feels terrible. He explains what happened as he hands the book to Sergio. "I'm really sorry," he apologizes. "I should have been more careful."

Sergio looks upset for a moment and Kurt is afraid he has made his friend very angry. Then Sergio sighs and says, "It's okay. The same thing could have happened to me."

Kurt feels relieved. He tells himself that he will never be so careless with someone else's property again.

That afternoon, when Kurt opens the door to his bedroom, he is greeted by a squeal from his four-year-old brother. Kenny is hiding something behind his back.

"What are you doing in here?" asks Kurt accusingly. "And what's that behind your back."

"Nothing," says Kenny weakly, tears rising in his eyes.

Kurt lunges forward, grabs Kenny by the arm and turns him around. Kenny is holding Kurt's newest model spacecraft, and it is broken.

"I'm sorry," wails Kenny. "I was just looking at it and it dropped. Don't be mad, Kurt!"

Kurt stares at the shattered hull and feels his temper flare. Then he remembers the comic book and Sergio's reaction. He sets his books on the bed, takes a deep breath, and gently tossles Kenny's hair. "Don't cry, Ken," he says. "We all make mistakes sometimes. Let's see if we can fix it."

Discussion Questions:
1. What are the moral values in this situation?
2. How would you feel if you were Sergio? What would you do?
3. What did Kurt learn from Sergio's reaction?
4. Have you ever forgiven someone for hurting you or one of your possessions? Explain.
5. Why is it a good idea to forgive sometimes?

On Moral Grounds
Writing, Sharing, and Discussion

Purpose:
To examine personal decisions that were made based on moral values.

Materials:
writing and drawing materials

Procedure:
Begin by reviewing the universal moral values examined so far by the students. Write a list on the board, *e.g.*:
Trustworthiness
Respect
Responsibility
Justice and Fairness
Caring
Citizenship

In your own words, explain one of the following assignments:

1. *I want you to think of an <u>ethical</u> (values) <u>dilemma</u> from you own life. Perhaps you had to make a decision that involved one of the values on the board. For example, maybe you knew that the decision would cause someone to either trust you or not trust you in the future. Or perhaps the decision involved taking responsibility for some action, or being fair in the way you judged a situation. Most of us face moral dilemmas from time to time.*

Once you have identified the dilemma, write about it. Describe the circumstances, what your choices were, and explain how you resolved the problem and why. If this dilemma is still going on now, describe how you are feeling about it and what you might do. If you'd rather, you may draw a picture of the situation — or you may both write and draw.

2. Your assignment is to describe in writing a behavior that you've <u>changed</u> based on moral grounds. Perhaps you used to tease certain people because of things about them that were different, and you've stopped doing that because it's wrong. Or maybe you used to cheat occasionally, but have decided to start taking responsibility for your own work. Have you become more honest? Trustworthy? Considerate of others? Why did you decide to make this change? Describe the change, what led up to it, and how it feels to have strengthened your character. If you'd rather, you may draw two pictures — one showing the old behavior and another illustrating the new behavior. Or you may both write and draw.

CHARACTER EDUCATION IN AMERICA'S SCHOOLS: Moral Reflection

Have the students share their papers in groups of three to five. Allow plenty of time for discussion. Give the students an opportunity to correct and rewrite their papers before placing the papers, along with illustrations, in a binder.

Discussion Questions:
1. What causes certain decisions to become difficult dilemmas?
2. What kind of questions can you ask yourself when you have a tough decision to make?
3. Was it hard to make the change you described?
4. How do you feel now about the decision or change you made?

Something I've Done (or Could Do) to Improve Our Community
A Sharing Circle

Purpose:
This circle encourages the students to describe how they can contribute to the betterment of the community, and to verbalize the importance of community involvement.

Introduce the Topic:
The topic for this session is, "Something I've Done (or Could Do) to Improve Our Community." Can you think of a time when you did something that you felt really helped, even in a small way, to improve the community we live in? Perhaps you improved the condition of your neighborhood by cleaning up yards, empty lots, and streets. Or perhaps you did something to help our environment—like try to use less water and electricity. Maybe you helped in an effort to find homes for stray animals or shelter for homeless people. Whatever you did, we would like to hear about it. If you can't think of something you've already done, perhaps you can think of something you would like to do in the future, either independently or with a group. Our topic is, "Something I've Done (or Could Do) to Improve Our Community."

Discussion Questions:
1. What ideas did you hear during this session that especially interested you? How can you find out more about those opportunities?
2. How do you feel when you do something that helps improve our community?
3. How can we encourage more people to get involved in improving the community?

Topic Variations:
A Problem in My Neighborhood That Needs To Be Solved

Something I've Done or Could Do to Improve Our World

A Character Trait I Admire in Others
A Sharing Circle

Purpose:
To identify admirable qualities and to explain how such qualities contribute to "good character."

Introduce the Topic
We have talked about a number of important character traits — qualities in ourselves and others that we value, such as honesty, loyalty, patience, caring, forgiveness, respectfulness, responsibility, and fairness. In this session, we're going to think of one quality that we particularly value. Our topic is, "A Character Trait I Admire in Others."

One way to do this is to think of one or two people whom you really like and respect. Then ask yourself what character trait really stands out in these people. You might decide that the strongest character trait they have is honesty. Perhaps they are always truthful, never try to avoid responsibility for their actions by lying, and tell you exactly what they think so you never have to wonder. Maybe you admire people who show a lot of caring and concern for others, try to be helpful, and go out of their way to do thoughtful things. Or perhaps you admire people who accept responsibility without hesitation, who are leaders, and who are the first to act when something needs to be done. Think about it for a few moments. Our topic is, "A Character Trait I Admire in Others."

Discussion Questions:
1. Why is it important to have good character?
2. How are good character traits developed?
3. What good qualities would you like people to recognize in you?
4. What character traits would you like to change?

Topic Variations:
A Character Trait I Would Like to Develop

Someone of Good Character Whom I Admire

One of My Strongest Character Traits

What Good Character Means to Me

I Made a Decision Based on My Values
A Sharing Circle

Purpose:
To become conscious of the role of values in guiding everyday decisions.

Introduce the Topic:
The topic today is, "I Made a Decision Based on My Values." Making this kind of decision is not an unusual event. We all make many choices daily because of things that are important to us or things we strongly believe in. Think of one example from your own experience and describe it to us. Maybe you decided to assist a classmate who was having trouble with a math problem — not because you had to, but because you believe that it is important to help others. Perhaps you decided to tell the truth about something, even though telling the truth caused someone to get angry at you. You did it because you value honesty. Or maybe you decided to clean up your trash after lunch because you want to show respect for the environment. Have you ever decided to keep a secret no matter what? Did you do it because you value being a trustworthy person? Have you ever reported a crime? Do you listen when someone else is speaking? Do you do these things because you know they are the responsible, respectful things to do? We all make many decisions every day. Tell us about one that was guided by a value. Our topic is, "I Made a Decision Based on My Values."

Discussion Questions:
1. How did you feel when you made the decision you described?
2. Why is it important to be guided by values?
3. How can you be sure that your values are the right ones?
4. Where do we learn our values?

Topic Variations:
A Value That Is Important to Me

Something I Can Do to Improve My Values

A Time When Strong Values Guided My Actions

The Moral Value That Gives Me the Most Trouble

I Did Something That Made Me Feel Like a Good Person
A Sharing Circle

Purpose:
To help the students identify actions that exemplify positive moral values; to describe how good feelings result from good behavior.

Introduce the Topic:
Our Sharing Circle topic today is, "I Did Something That Made Me Feel Like a Good Person." We do many things that cause us to feel good about ourselves. Sometimes we do them spontaneously and sometimes we plan them in advance. Tell us about something you did that resulted in positive feelings. You may have done it for yourself, or for another person — or perhaps it was for an animal or the environment. Other people may have known about what you did, or you may have kept it to yourself until now.

Maybe you were honest with someone, even though it was difficult. Perhaps you completed a difficult assignment on time and did the very best job you could. Or maybe you showed kindness toward a person who was in trouble. Did you report a crime, or explain the importance of a law to your younger brother or sister? Did you call a play fairly in sports, or settle a conflict fairly? Think about it for a few moments. The topic is, "I Did Something That Made Me Feel Like a Good Person."

Summary Discussion Questions:
1. What kinds of actions caused us to feel like good people?
2. When we feel we have done something good, is it important to get recognition from someone else? Why or why not?
3. How do you know the difference between good and bad actions?
4. What is your conscience? When your conscience bothers you, what does that mean?

Topic Variations:
I Did Something That Made Me Feel Like a Bad Person

A Time I Had a Fight With My Conscience

I Did It Because My Conscience Told Me To

A Time I Put Myself in Someone Else's Shoes
A Sharing Circle

Purpose:
To describe instances of perspective-taking; to explain how perspective taking contributes to interpersonal understanding and problem solving.

Introduce the Topic:
Our topic for this session is, "A Time I Put Myself in Someone Else's Shoes." Do you know what that expression means? Putting yourself in someone else's shoes means seeing and feeling things from that person's point of view. Think of a time when you tried very hard to understand how someone was thinking or feeling by imagining what it would be like to be in that person's shoes. Maybe you had a conflict with a friend and tried to see the conflict the way he did. Or maybe you wanted to better understand how a situation looked to someone from a different culture, so you asked questions and listened carefully to that person's answers. Have you ever tried to understand what it would be like to be blind, or to have some other kind of disability? Have you ever tried to understand how someone feels who cannot speak your language? Taking the perspective of other people helps us to understand them. Tell us what you learned by walking in someone else's shoes. Our topic is, "A Time I Put Myself in Someone Else's Shoes."

Summary Discussion Questions:
1. How did it feel to put yourself in someone else's shoes?
2. What do you need to do in order to understand another person's point of view?
3. How does putting ourselves in the shoes of others help us solve problems and resolve conflicts?
4. How do you feel when a person refuses to understand where you are coming from?
5. What would the world be like if people and countries were unwilling to understand each other's points of view?

Topic Variations:
A Time Someone Understood My Point of View

A Time My Point of View Was Misunderstood

Literature Connections

One of the easiest, most enjoyable and effective ways to teach moral values is through literature. The books annotated on the following pages were selected because they relate directly to the six core values around which this book is organized. You should have no trouble locating these titles; all are popular books, readily available through libraries and bookstores. Each of the entries is coded to indicate grade level — primary (P), intermediate (I), or upper (U).

Characters in literature offer refreshing alternatives to the heroes and role models children are exposed to on television and the pages of *People* magazine. And since good literature can always be counted on to richly reflect aspects of the human condition, the fact that most of the characters are fictional is of minor importance.

Whether the students are reading on their own or listening as you bring the story to life, encourage them to analyze the motivations and moral struggles of the characters in the story. Ask questions, facilitate discussion, and occasionally have students act out the story's central dilemma, decision point, or consummate moment.

Discussion Questions:
—*What universal moral values played a role in this story?*
—*Which behaviors in this story were good/right?*
—*Which behaviors violated a universal moral value and were therefore wrong? Which universal moral values were violated?*
—*What has this character done that you admire? What has s/he done that you would want to imitate?*
—*What is the right thing to do about this issue (going on right now in the story)?*
—*Who is doing what to whom and why?*
—*What is the evidence in the situation? How do you evaluate the evidence? How do you apply the evidence?*
—*Can you think of a similar incident in real life? What principles from that incident can you apply to this one?*
—*What are possible alternative solutions/actions in this situation? What are the probable consequences of each action/solution?*
—*What is the best action/solution?*

Literature Connections:
Trustworthiness

Brooks, Bruce, *What Hearts*, New York, HarperCollins, 1993.
Four short stories are woven together to offer a perceptive picture of Asa's development as a person from age 6 to 12. The trauma of his parents' divorce, a move, a new stepfather, and important decisions such as choosing between the spotlight in a class performance and loyalty to a new friend are events that assist in Asa's character development. (U)

Bunting, Eve, *Summer Wheels*, New York, Harcourt Brace, 1993.
A friendly man fixes up bicycles and lends them to neighborhood kids for free. A new kid, who calls himself "Abraham Lincoln," thinks that anyone fool enough to give something for nothing deserves to lose it. Using the only means he knows to get acceptance and friendship, the boy eventually returns the bike. (I)

Duvoisin, Roger, *Petunia*, New York, Alfred A. Knopf, 1950.
A goose named Petunia finds a book and, because she overhears someone say that books make you wise, she pretends to know everything. When all the other animals go to her for advice, she gives them bad counsel and finally injures herself and her friends when she reads, "Candies," on a box labeled, "Firecrackers." (P)

Griffin, Judith Berry, *Phoebe The Spy*, New York, Scholastic, 1977.
In 1776, a thirteen-year-old black girl disguises herself as General Washington's housekeeper to guard his life from an unknown killer. This is a true story of courage and loyalty during the American Revolution. (I,U)

Martin, Rafe, *The Rough-Faced Girl*, New York, Putnam, 1993.
This is an Algonquin Indian version of the Cinderella story. Two vain and arrogant sisters try to prove that they can see the "invisible being," but are dishonest in their descriptions. Their sister, whose face and body are scarred from sitting and tending the fire, sees the beauty of the invisible being in nature around her, and is successful. (P,I,U)

Palmer, Joan, *Dog Facts*, New York, 1991, Marboro Books Corporation.
This factual book answers hundreds of questions about dogs, giving insights into every aspect of dog character. It has a dog directory of breeds, their descriptions, and illustrations. (I,U)

San Souci, Robert D., *The Samurai's Daughter*, New York, Dial, 1993.
A retelling of a Japanese legend, this is the tale of a girl named Tokyo who sets out to find her exiled father by climbing mountains, crossing the ocean, and battling a sea serpent. She is determined to contribute to the Samurai virtues of courage, endurance, and the warrior's duty to protect the weak — even as she is taught to be ladylike and genteel. (I,U)

Sharmat, Marjorie Weinman, *A Big Fat Enormous Lie*, New York, 1978, E.P. Dutton.
When Father asks if he ate the jar of cookies, a small boy tells a lie and says no. His troubles begin as the lie grows into a terrible monster that haunts him continuously until the boy confronts his parents with the truth. (P)

Steig, William, *Dr. DeSoto*, New York, Farrar, Straus & Giroux, 1982.
Dr. DeSoto is a mouse-dentist who takes a risk and decides to help out a fox with a toothache. When he realizes that the fox plans to eat him, he must use his head to avert the plan. (P)

Respect

Bedard, Michael, *Emily*, New York, 1992, Doubleday.
This is a fictional story of an encounter between a young girl and the poet Emily Dickenson. The little girl is asked to play the piano for "the Myth," a nickname given to Emily by the neighborhood people. This book introduces children to the poet and gives some insights into the her odd behavior. (P,I,U)

Cohen, Barbara, *Molly's Pilgrim*, New York, Lothrup, Lee & Shepard, 1983.
Molly and her parents emigrated from Russia to the United States to seek religious freedom, but Molly is unhappy about her clothes, her customs, and her English. When Molly's class makes pilgrim dolls for Thanksgiving, her Jewish mother dresses Molly's doll as she was dressed before leaving Russia. Molly's classmates learn to respect her as a modern day pilgrim. (I)

Gherman, Beverly, *E.B. White: Some Writer!*, New York, Atheneum, 1992.
This biography of the quiet man who wrote Charlotte's Web and many other enduring pieces of children's literature takes us through his life as a shy child, awkward adolescent, and unsure young adult who found pleasure in writing. The author allows us into his life and genius, giving us a glimpse of a person many consider an old friend. (U)

Markun, Patricia Malone, *The Little Painter of Sabana Grande*, New York, 1993, Bradbury.
This is based on a true story about the village of Las Tablas in Mexico. It tells of a young boy named Fernando Espino who has no paper on which to use his freshly made, natural paints, so he paints the smooth white walls of his family's adobe house. Soon all the villagers ask him to paint their homes as well. (P)

McKissack, Patricia C. and Frederick, *Ida B. Wells-Burnett: a Voice Against Violence*, 1991, Enslow.
This is the story of a woman who was born a slave and who dedicates her life to improving race relations through her work as a journalist and helping to establish the NAACP. (I)

Rood, Peter and Connie, *Ahyoka and the Talking Leaves*, New York, Lothrup, 1992.
Ahyoka is the daughter of Sequoyah, a Cherokee who creates a written language for his people. She acts as his assistant in this endeavor, believing in her father when no one else does. This book is a fictionalized biography of Ahyoka. (I,U)

Sandburg, Carl, illustrated by James Daugherty, *Abe Lincoln Grows Up*, New York, Harcourt, 1940.
This book is taken from the beginning chapters of Sandburs's *Abraham Lincoln: The Prairie Years*, and portrays Lincoln's boyhood. (I,U)

Schwartz, David M., *Supergrandpa*, New York, Lothrop, 1991.
In 1951, 66-year-old Gustaf Hakansson wanted to enter the 1,094-mile bicycle race around Sweden, but he was considered too old for such a strenuous competition. In this fictionalized account, Hakansson races day and night, finishes the course, and wins — not the race, but the admiration and respect of his countrymen. (I,U)

Skira-Venturi, Rosabianca, *A Weekend with Leonardo Da Vinci*, New York, 1992, Rizzoli.
Hillary, age 10, takes a tour of Da Vinci's rooms at the castle of the Amboise and learns about his inventions and ideas. The text is told from two perspectives: first person, through the artist's eyes, and third person, as Hillary tells about the pictures. Full color reproductions and photographs enhance the text. (I,U)

Stanley, Diane, and Vennema, Peter, *Charles Dickens: The Man Who Had Great Expectations*, New York, 1993, Morrow.
This is the story of the famous English author whose books are based on his own experiences and observations when, as a child, he had to quit school to find work. (I, U)

Responsibility

Arnold, Tedd, *The Signmaker's Assistant*, New York, Dial, 1992.
Norman, the signmaker's assistant, paints many signs that create chaos in town. When the signmaker leaves on a trip, school closes, people dump garbage at the grocery store, and cars are detoured through a home. The people realize their foolishness in following the new signs and the boy realizes the need for responsibility in what he does. (P,I)

Bulla, Clyde Robert, *Shoeshine Girl*, New York, Crowell, 1975.
One summer Sara Ida goes to live with Aunt Claudia who is instructed not to give her any money. She gets a job in a shoeshine stand and succeeds in her work, taking full responsibility for the stand when the owner is hurt in an accident. (I,U)

Byars, Betsy, *The Summer of the Swans*, New York, Viking, 1970.
Sara is preoccupied with her mood swings, from elation one moment to tears the next, until one night her mentally retarded younger brother, Charlie, disappears. Sara searches dense woods and rough fields, and, in anguish, turns to Joe Melby, whom she despised only the day before, and together they find Charlie. After that day, Sara knows that she will never be the same.

Cooney, Barbara, *Miss Rumphius*, New York, Viking, 1982.
Miss Rumphius travels the world and returns to live by the sea as she planned. However, she also wants to make the world more beautiful, so she plants beautiful lupines all over the fields. Thus, she becomes known as the lupine lady. (P,I)

The Earthworks Group, *50 Simple Things Kids Can Do to Save the Earth*, New York, Scholastic, 1990.
Experiments, facts, and exciting things for kids to do to preserve the environment, like being a water leak detective, joining the "Heat-Busters," and adopting a stream. (P.I.U.)

Irwin, Hadley, *The Lilith Summer*, New York, The Feminist Press, 1979.
Twelve-year-old Ellen agrees to spend a whole summer of her life "lady-sitting" with 77-year-old Lilith Adams to earn money for a ten-speed bicycle. Ellen could never have imagined how much she would grow to love and respect Lilith's strength, wisdom, and independence while sharing experiences and adventures with her. (U)

Joyce, William, *Bently and Egg*, New York, Scholastic, 1992.
In this story about friendship and responsibility, Kack Kack the duck asks Bently the frog to watch her precious egg while she goes to visit her sister. Bently learns the seriousness of his task when his charge is "eggnapped" and he engages in many adventures to retrieve the egg safely. (P)

Levine, Susan A., *Save Our Planet: 52 Easy Things Kids Can Do Now*, New York, Parachute Press, 1990.
This book of earth-saving activities includes "Garbage Actions," "Water Actions," "Air Actions," "Animal Actions," "Earth Actions," and "For Kids Only Actions." (P.I.U.)

Madden, Don, *The Wartville Wizard*, New York, Aladdin/Macmillan, 1993.
An old man fights a town of litterbugs by magically sending each piece of trash back to the person who dropped it and making it stick to him or her. The people of Wartville learn an important lesson about responsibility. (P,I)

NK Lawn & Garden Co., *My First Garden Book*, New York, Avon Books, 1992.
Each of the 17 planting projects in this step-by-step guide starts off with a story or a poem that is then recreated in the garden that follows. Imaginative gardening projects such as the "Flower Castle Garden" result in representations of the gardens in the preceding stories.

Schwartz, Linda, *Earth Book for Kids: Activities to Help Heal the Environment*, Santa Barbara, The Learning Works, 1990.
Fascinating facts and creative ideas for activities to help kids become better acquainted with their environment and learn to care for the earth. (I,U)

Sunset Publishing Co., *Best Kids' Garden Book*, Menlo Park, CA, Sunset Publishing Co., 1992.
This all-round gardening book for children covers everything from planting seeds to painting with potatoes. It gives step-by-step projects that emphasize the fun of gardening while giving guidelines for the beginning gardener in how to care for plants. (P, I, U)

Caring

Byars, Betsy, *The Pinballs*, New York, Harper & Row, 1977.
Three lonely and alienated children are thrown together in a foster home. Harvey's drunken father ran over him with a car and broke both his legs and Carlie and Thomas J. figure they are all pinballs: they don't get to settle where they want to. But all three eventually find love and caring with each other and their new foster parents. (I,U)

Cherry, Lynne, *The Great Kapok Tree*, San Diego, Harcourt Brace Jovanovich, 1990.
A man enters the rain forest and chops away at a great Kapok tree until he tires. Sitting down to rest, the man falls asleep and is visited in his dreams by all of the rain forest animals that depend on the tree for life. When the man awakens, he decides not to cut down the tree. (P.I.U.)

Herriot, James, *The Market Square Dog*, New York, Scholastic, 1989.
A seriously injured stray dog is rescued by a policeman and saved by a kind veterinarian. However, no one chooses to adopt him from the pound. Then policeman decides to take the dog home for his children. (P,I)

Sharmat, Marjorie Weinman, *Gladys Told Me To Meet Her Here*, New York, Harper & Row, 1970.
A little boy's thoughts run wild as he waits for his best friend, Gladys, at the park. As he wanders around, he worries that she is lost; then gets mad when he thinks she is just late. When he returns to the spot where they agreed to meet, he finds her. (P)

Sabuda, Robert, *Saint Valentine*, New York, Atheneum, 1992.
This is a vignette of the compassionate life of the physician and Christian priest, Valentine. It is the story of a miracle that happens when he cares for a jailer's daughter, restoring her sight with a crocus he sends to her on her execution day. (I)

Yoshi, Andrew Clements, *Big Al*, New York, Scholastic, 1988.
Big Al is a very big, scary fish who works hard to make friends with other fish in the salty sea. He wraps himself up in seaweed, puffing up to make the other fish laugh, and even changes color to match a school of tiny fish. But the other fish are afraid to make friends with Al, until he saves them from a fisherman's net and gets caught himself. (P)

L'Engle, Madeleine, *A Wrinkle in Time*, New York, Farrar, Straus and Giroux, 1962.
Meg Murray and her precocious little brother, Charles Wallace, seek comfort and support in each other, and set off to find and rescue their scientist father. In this science fiction adventure, the children learn the strongest gift of all, the power of love, which saves them and their father from the evil force. (U)

White, E.B., *Charlotte's Web*, New York, Harper &Row, 1952.
In this beloved children's classic, a little girl named Fern saves the life of a runt piglet named Wilbur. Thus begins a story of loyalty and friendship between Wilbur and a lovely grey spider named Charlotte. (I,U)

Rylant, Cynthia, *Missing May*, Orchard/A Richard Jackson Book, 1992.
Uncle Ob and Aunt May gladly take in 12-year-old Summer when her mother dies. However, when May dies, Ob cannot do anything but grieve. Summer fears that Ob is losing the will to live and frantically tries to find it for him. This story deals with love's capacity to make life worthwhile. (U)

Justice and Fairness

Brandt, Deith, *Rosa Parks: Fight for Freedom*, Troll Associates, 1993.
A biography of the woman who decided that being black was not a good enough reason to relinquish her bus seat to a white man. Her actions led to the desegregation of buses in Montgomery, Alabama in the 1960s. (I,U)

Brown, Marc, *Arthur's April Fool*, New York, Little Brown, 1983.
Binky Barnes takes Arthur's favorite pen and threatens to punch him out. Authur uses cunning to get the best of the bully. (P)

Byars, Betsy, *The Eighteenth Emergency*, Viking/Penguin, 1973.
Benjie "Mouse" Fawley flees from Marv, the toughest kid in the school, after writing Marv's name under a Neanderthal man on a school chart. His best friend, Ezzie, has developed sure-fire solutions to 17 emergencies, like how to survive attacks of stampeding elephants and hungry crocodiles, but has no solution for this 18th emergency! (U)

Carrick, Carrol, *What a Wimp!*, New York, 1983, Clarion Books.
It all starts when Barney's mom decides to move them to the country and Barney meets the bully, Lenny Coots. Although his mother, older brother, and teacher sympathize, Barney has to figure out for himself how to deal with the bully. (I,U)

Chapman, Carol, *Herbie's Troubles*, New York, 1981, E.P. Dutton.
Six-and-one-half-year-old Herbie likes school until he meets Jimmy John who terrorizes the sandbox, the classroom, and the bathroom! Following the advice of friends gets Jimmy into more trouble so Jimmy solves the problem in his own way. (P)

Estes, Eleanor, *The Hundred Dresses*, San Diego, Harcourt Brace Jovanovich, 1944.
Although Wanda Petronski wears the same faded-blue dress to school every day, she tells the other girls that she has a hundred dresses. The girls make fun of her daily until one day Wanda doesn't come to school anymore. The class finds out about her hundred dresses and learns an important lesson. (I)

Gantos, *Rotten Ralph*, Boston, Houghton Mifflin, 1976.
Sarah's cat, Ralph, makes fun of her when she practices ballet and ruins her party by taking a bite out of every one of her cookies, among other "rotten" things. The family finally leaves Ralph at a circus where he has to work and sleep in a cage. Ralph learns his lesson and returns home penitent. (P,I)

Henkes, Kevin, *Chrysanthemum*, New York, Greenwillow, 1991.
The girls in Chrysanthemum's kindergarten class make fun of her name and tease her mercilessly until their beloved music teacher Mrs. Twinkle decides to name her baby, Chrysanthemum. (P)

Hoffman, Mary, *Amazing Grace*, New York, Dial, 1991.
Although her classmates say that she cannot play Peter Pan in the school play because she is black and a girl, Grace discovers that she can do anything she sets her mind to. (P,I)

Paterson, Katherine, *The Great Gilly Hopkins*, New York, Thomas Y. Crowell, 1978
This Newberry Honor book tells about a bright eleven-year-old girl named Gilly who is rebellious, manipulative, and hostile as a result of being abandoned at age three by her young mother. She schemes against everyone who tries to be friendly to her until her newest foster mother pours unstinting love on her, breaking down Gilly's defenses. From then on, Gilly decides to make her life different. (U)

Seuss, Dr., *The Sneetches*, New York, Random House, 1961.
This humorous but poignant story-poem reveals conflicts between its characters that stem from individual differences. The Star-Belly Sneetches snub the Plain Bellies until a salesman comes to town with a star stamping machine, throwing confusion into the community and, ultimately, awareness of their folly. (P,I,U)

Taylor, Mildred, *Roll of Thunder, Hear My Cry*, New York, Dial, 1976.
This Newberry Award winner is the story of a turbulent year in the life of a girl named Cassie and her family, who are victims of night riders, burnings and public humiliations because they are black. (U)

Taylor, Theodore, *The Cay*, Doubleday, 1969.
After the Germans torpedo the boat on which Phillip and his mother are travelling during World War II, Phillip finds himself blind and stranded on a small Caribbean island with a black islander named Timothy. This is the story of their survival, and of Phillip's efforts to understand the dignified, wise, and loving old man whose race and culture had once inspired Phillip's hatred. (U)

Wilhelm, Hans, *Tyrone the Horrible*, New York, 1988, Scholastic.
A little dinosaur named Boland lives in a great swamp forest with his family and friends and is picked on all the time by a big dinosaur named Tyrone. Boland tries to follow the advice of others but always ends up getting punched, teased, or hurt. Finally Boland thinks up a solution which teaches Tyrone a lesson. (P)

Citizenship

Ashabranner, Brent, *A Memorial for Mr. Lincoln*, New York, Putnam, 1992.
This book allows children to look at our nation's heritage and pride through a quiet history of the Lincoln Monument. It starts with highlights of Lincoln's presidency and continues through the construction of the memorial and the design and completion of the statue. (U)

Bates, Katherine Lee, *America the Beautiful*, New York, Atheneum, 1993.
Highlighting landscapes that span the U.S. from coast to coast, Neil Waldman has illustrated the first verse of this poem. Inspired by a view from Pike's Peak, Katherine Bates wrote the poem over one hundred years ago. The music, created two years after the poem, is provided on the end pages. (P,I,U)

Chalofsky, M. et. al., *Changing Places: A Kid's View of Shelter Living*, Mt. Rainier, MD, Gryphon House, 1992.
Eight children living in a family shelter in Virginia share their words and real experiences to help other homeless children realize that they aren't alone and their feelings are shared. The book gives insight into a variety of situations that create homelessness and challenges readers to become involved in community programs that aid homeless families. (I,U)

Cohn, Amy L., ed, *From Sea to Shining Sea: A Treasury of American Folklore and Folksongs*, New York, Scholastic, 1993.
A collection of over 140 American folktales, poems, essays, and songs, this book is divided into 15 chapters placed in historical context, each representing a specific period in American history. It is filled with traditional and nontraditional folklore embracing all races, and reflecting the diversity of America. (P,I,U)

Durell, Ann and Sachs, Marilyn, Eds., *The Big Book for Peace*, New York, Dutton, 1990.
Stories, pictures, poems and songs representing the work of more than thirty of the best known authors and illustrators of children's books, this volume is about the wisdom of peace among next-door neighbors and among people living in different lands; about harmony among sisters and brothers and among people of different races; about understanding among those separated by beliefs and by generations. It lends itself to discussion of issues and community involvement. (P,I,U)

Fisher, Leonard Everett, *Stars and Stripes: Our National Flag*, New York, Holiday House, 1993.
The origin, dates and purpose of flags that have been important in U.S. history are placed throughout this informational book, while the text of the Pledge of Allegiance provides the framework for their display. The history of the Pledge is appended at the end.

Goldin, Barbara Diamond, *Fire! The Beginnings of the Labor Movement*, New York, Viking, 1992.
Rosie is 11 and wants to leave school to work in a garment factory on New York's Lower East Side. After she witnesses the 1911 Triangle Shirtwaist fire, she works to better working conditions. (I,U)

Krull, Kathleen, collector and arranger, *Gonna Sing My Head Off!*, New York, Knopf, 1992.
This is a collection of American folk songs carefully selected to represent regional and cultural diversity. A brief note accompanies each song, and all songs are arranged for both piano and guitar. (P,I,U)

O'Neal, Zibby, *A Long Way to Go: The Story of Women's Right to Vote*, New York, Viking, 1990.
In 1917, during World War I, ten-year-old Lila joins her grandmother in the fight to gain women's suffrage, even though her parents do not approve. (I,U)

Van Raven, Pieter, *Harpoon Island*, New York, Macmillan, 1989.
Set on a Massachusetts island just before the United States enters World War I, this story portrays how bigotry and prejudice affect the lives of a German-American teacher and his young son, who is unable to speak. (U)

Wood, Douglas, *Old Turtle*, Duluth, MN, Pfeifer-Hamilton, 1992.
In this fable for all ages, wise and strong Old Turtle quietly helps other animals realize that the earth is made up of a variety of beings, all of which need to live harmoniously if the planet is to survive. The story prompts discussion about pressing social and political issues such as feminism, sex-role stereotypes, images of God, creation stories, environmental ethics, and the need for peace. (P,I,U)

Jalmar Press and Innerchoice Publishing are happy to announce

a collaborative effort under which all Innerchoice titles will now be distributed

only through Jalmar Press.

To request the latest catalog of our joint resources for use by teachers, counselors

and other care-givers to empower children to develop inner-directed living and

learning skills

call us at: (800) 662-9662

or fax us at: (310) 816-3092

or send us a card at: P.O. Box 1185, Torrance, CA 90505

We're eager to serve you and the students you work with.

By the way, Jalmar Press has a new series coming up that can give you all the necessary tools to teach character traits to all your students. It's called

CHARACTER BUILDERS
BY
DR. MICHELE BORBA

and is aimed at grades K - 6.

Three titles will be available in spring, 1998 and another three in fall, 1998.
Write or call for the latest information or to place your order.

More Products from INNERCHOICE PUBLISHING

New products are routinely added to our collection of books and materials for counselors and teachers. Here are a few samples.

THE SHARING CIRCLE HANDBOOK
Topics for Teaching Self-Awareness, Communication, and Social Skills

All students need a safe place to dialogue —to share their feelings, thoughts, and concerns with supportive peers and an attentive adult. Each of the handbook's over 100 Sharing Circles includes a list of skill areas addressed by the topic, suggestions for introducing the topic to students, and questions to ask during the summary discussion. Step-by-step instructions for leading Sharing Circles are included, along with guidelines for developing student leadership. Recommended for use with students of all ages, including students at risk of dropping out, underachievers, gifted students, and other special populations.

PEACE PATROL
Creating a New Generation of Problem Solvers and Peacemakers

Teach *all* students to be effective problem solvers and positive decision makers by replicating the highly acclaimed, award-winning Peace Patrol program in your school! This organizational guide plots a clear course for both elementary and middle schools in how to get started, win faculty and administrator support, and recruit and train students. Includes activities, handouts, forms, and resources. This is more than peer mediation—this is moral development on the fast track!

GETTING ALONG
Activities for Teaching Cooperation, Responsibility, and Respect

Sixty-five instantly usable social skills activities—discussions, role plays, games, simulations, and worksheets—designed to develop: appreciation for individual differences; inclusion, cooperation, and interdependence among students; skills for cooperative problem solving, communication, and conflict management. An excellent resource for promoting the values of respect and responsibility.

TOGETHER, I CAN
Cooperative Learning Activities for Counselors and Teachers

Carefully designed small-group strategies that foster social skills, communication skills, empathy, problem solving, and higher-order thinking skills. The collaborative models outlined and described provide everything you need to add cooperative strategies to your repertoire. Includes a theory-based introduction, 20 cooperative learning strategies, and over 50 interdisciplinary and subject-specific lessons in Language Arts, Science, Social Science, Health, and Problem Solving.

TEACHING THE SKILLS OF CONFLICT RESOLUTION
Activities and Strategies for Counseling and Teaching

This thoroughly useful activity book will help you reduce classroom and school conflicts through the creation of a more peaceful, cooperative learning environment, and give students tools to resolve and learn from conflicts when they occur. Activities help students deal with their feelings; appreciate and include others; practice effective communication, problem-solving and decision-making; reduce stress, and learn specific conflict resolution and peer-mediation skills.